D1824310

Virtual Desktop Infrastructure Monitoring Complete Self-Assessment Guide

The guidance in this Self-Assessment is based on Virtual Desktop Infrastructure Monitoring best practices and standards in business process architecture, design and quality management. The guidance is also based on the professional judgment of the individual collaborators listed in the Acknowledgments.

Notice of rights

Trademarks

Table of Contents

About The Art of Service

The Art of Service, Business Process Architects since 2000, is dedicated to helping stakeholders achieve excellence.

Defining, designing, creating, and implementing a process to solve a stakeholders challenge or meet an objective is the most valuable role… In EVERY group, company, organization and department.

Unless you're talking a one-time, single-use project, there should be a process. Whether that process is managed and implemented by humans, AI, or a combination of the two, it needs to be designed by someone with a complex enough perspective to ask the right questions.

Someone capable of asking the right questions and step back and say, 'What are we really trying to accomplish here? And is there a different way to look at it?'

With The Art of Service's Standard Requirements Self-Assessments, we empower people who can do just that — whether their title is marketer, entrepreneur, manager, salesperson, consultant, Business Process Manager, executive assistant, IT Manager, CIO etc... —they are the people who rule the future. They are people who watch the process as it happens, and ask the right questions to make the process work better.

Contact us when you need any support with this Self-Assessment and any help with templates, blue-prints and examples of standard documents you might need:

http://theartofservice.com
service@theartofservice.com

Acknowledgments

This checklist was developed under the auspices of The Art of Service, chaired by Gerardus Blokdyk.

Representatives from several client companies participated in the preparation of this Self-Assessment.

Our deepest gratitude goes out to Matt Champagne, Ph.D. Surveys Expert, for his invaluable help and advise in structuring the Self Assessment.

In addition, we are thankful for the design and printing services provided.

Included Resources - how to access

Included with your purchase of the book is the Virtual Desktop Infrastructure Monitoring Self-Assessment Spreadsheet Dashboard which contains all questions and Self-Assessment areas and auto-generates insights, graphs, and project RACI planning - all with examples to get you started right away.

How? Simply send an email to
access@theartofservice.com
with this books' title in the subject to get the Virtual Desktop Infrastructure Monitoring Self Assessment Tool right away.

You will receive the following contents with New and Updated specific criteria:
- The latest quick edition of the book in PDF
- The latest complete edition of the book in PDF, which criteria correspond to the criteria in...
- The Self-Assessment Excel Dashboard, and...
- Example pre-filled Self-Assessment Excel Dashboard to get familiar with results generation
- ...plus an extra, special, resource that helps you with project

managing.

INCLUDES LIFETIME SELF ASSESSMENT UPDATES

Every self assessment comes with Lifetime Updates and Lifetime Free Updated Books. Lifetime Updates is an industry-first feature which allows you to receive verified self assessment updates, ensuring you always have the most accurate information at your fingertips.

Get it now- you will be glad you did - do it now, before you forget.

Send an email to **access@theartofservice.com** with this books' title in the subject to get the Virtual Desktop Infrastructure Monitoring Self Assessment Tool right away.

Your feedback is invaluable to us

If you recently bought this book, we would love to hear from you! You can do this by writing a review on amazon (or the online store where you purchased this book) about your last purchase! As part of our continual service improvement process, we love to hear real client experiences and feedback.

How does it work?
To post a review on Amazon, just log in to your account and click on the Create Your Own Review button (under Customer Reviews) of the relevant product page. You can find examples of product reviews in Amazon. If you purchased from another online store, simply follow their procedures.

What happens when I submit my review?
Once you have submitted your review, send us an email at review@theartofservice.com with the link to your review so we can properly thank you for your feedback.

Purpose of this Self-Assessment

This Self-Assessment has been developed to improve understanding of the requirements and elements of Virtual Desktop Infrastructure Monitoring, based on best practices and standards in business process architecture, design and quality management.

It is designed to allow for a rapid Self-Assessment to determine how closely existing management practices and procedures correspond to the elements of the Self-Assessment.

The criteria of requirements and elements of Virtual Desktop Infrastructure Monitoring have been rephrased in the format of a Self-Assessment questionnaire, with a seven-criterion scoring system, as explained in this document.

In this format, even with limited background knowledge of Virtual Desktop Infrastructure Monitoring, a manager can quickly review existing operations to determine how they measure up to the standards. This in turn can serve as the starting point of a 'gap analysis' to identify management tools or system elements that might usefully be implemented in the organization to help improve overall performance.

How to use the Self-Assessment

On the following pages are a series of questions to identify to what extent your Virtual Desktop Infrastructure Monitoring initiative is complete in comparison to the requirements set in standards.

To facilitate answering the questions, there is a space in front of each question to enter a score on a scale of '1' to '5'.

1 Strongly Disagree

2 Disagree

3 Neutral

4 Agree

5 Strongly Agree

Read the question and rate it with the following in front of mind:

'In my belief, the answer to this question is clearly defined'.

There are two ways in which you can choose to interpret this statement;
1.   how aware are you that the answer to the question is

clearly defined

2. for more in-depth analysis you can choose to gather evidence and confirm the answer to the question. This obviously will take more time, most Self-Assessment users opt for the first way to interpret the question and dig deeper later on based on the outcome of the overall Self-Assessment.

A score of '1' would mean that the answer is not clear at all, where a '5' would mean the answer is crystal clear and defined. Leave emtpy when the question is not applicable or you don't want to answer it, you can skip it without affecting your score. Write your score in the space provided.

After you have responded to all the appropriate statements in each section, compute your average score for that section, using the formula provided, and round to the nearest tenth. Then transfer to the corresponding spoke in the Virtual Desktop Infrastructure Monitoring Scorecard on the second next page of the Self-Assessment.

Your completed Virtual Desktop Infrastructure Monitoring Scorecard will give you a clear presentation of which Virtual Desktop Infrastructure Monitoring areas need attention.

Virtual Desktop Infrastructure Monitoring
Scorecard Example

Example of how the finalized Scorecard can look like:

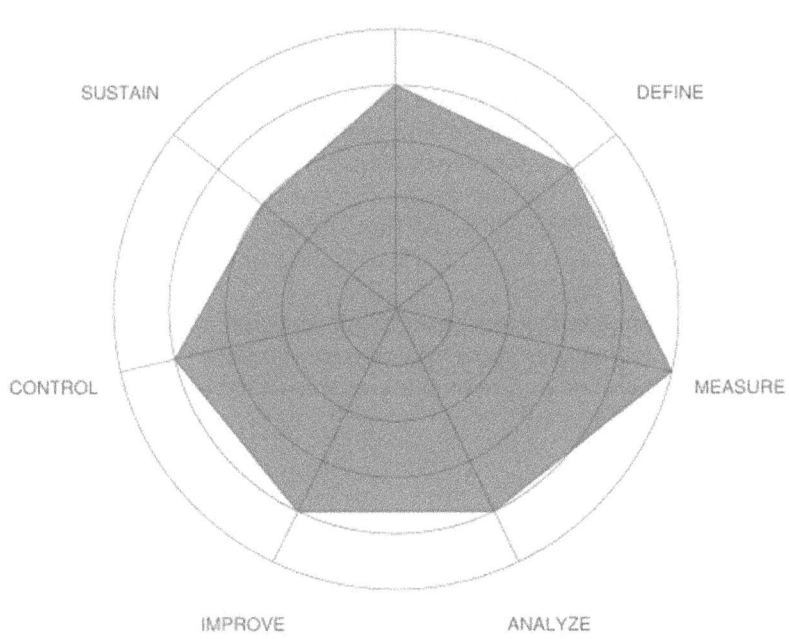

Virtual Desktop Infrastructure Monitoring
Scorecard

Your Scores:

BEGINNING OF THE SELF-ASSESSMENT:

CRITERION #1: RECOGNIZE

INTENT: Be aware of the need for change. Recognize that there is an unfavorable variation, problem or symptom.

In my belief, the answer to this question is clearly defined:

5 Strongly Agree

4 Agree

3 Neutral

2 Disagree

1 Strongly Disagree

1. Is it clear when you think of the day ahead of you what activities and tasks you need to complete?
<--- Score

2. Who had the original idea?
<--- Score

3. Does our organization need more Virtual Desktop Infrastructure Monitoring education?

<--- Score

4. What do we need to start doing?
<--- Score

5. Who defines the rules in relation to any given issue?
<--- Score

6. What information do users need?
<--- Score

7. What are the business objectives to be achieved with Virtual Desktop Infrastructure Monitoring?
<--- Score

8. How do you identify the kinds of information that you will need?
<--- Score

9. Who needs to know about Virtual Desktop Infrastructure Monitoring ?
<--- Score

10. Are there any specific expectations or concerns about the Virtual Desktop Infrastructure Monitoring team, Virtual Desktop Infrastructure Monitoring itself?
<--- Score

11. Who else hopes to benefit from it?
<--- Score

12. What should be considered when identifying available resources, constraints, and deadlines?
<--- Score

13. How are you going to measure success?

<--- Score

14. How do you assess your Virtual Desktop Infrastructure Monitoring workforce capability and capacity needs, including skills, competencies, and staffing levels?
<--- Score

15. Will it solve real problems?
<--- Score

16. Cloud management for Virtual Desktop Infrastructure Monitoring do we really need one?
<--- Score

17. Are there Virtual Desktop Infrastructure Monitoring problems defined?
<--- Score

18. Why do we need to keep records?
<--- Score

19. Are there recognized Virtual Desktop Infrastructure Monitoring problems?
<--- Score

20. What is the smallest subset of the problem we can usefully solve?
<--- Score

21. What problems are you facing and how do you consider Virtual Desktop Infrastructure Monitoring will circumvent those obstacles?
<--- Score

22. Can Management personnel recognize the

monetary benefit of Virtual Desktop Infrastructure Monitoring?

<--- Score

23. Consider your own Virtual Desktop Infrastructure Monitoring project. what types of organizational problems do you think might be causing or affecting your problem, based on the work done so far?

<--- Score

24. What vendors make products that address the Virtual Desktop Infrastructure Monitoring needs?

<--- Score

25. Think about the people you identified for your Virtual Desktop Infrastructure Monitoring project and the project responsibilities you would assign to them. what kind of training do you think they would need to perform these responsibilities effectively?

<--- Score

26. Does Virtual Desktop Infrastructure Monitoring create potential expectations in other areas that need to be recognized and considered?

<--- Score

27. How do we Identify specific Virtual Desktop Infrastructure Monitoring investment and emerging trends?

<--- Score

28. What situation(s) led to this Virtual Desktop Infrastructure Monitoring Self Assessment?

<--- Score

29. What are the expected benefits of Virtual Desktop Infrastructure Monitoring to the business?
<--- Score

30. How can auditing be a preventative security measure?
<--- Score

31. What tools and technologies are needed for a custom Virtual Desktop Infrastructure Monitoring project?
<--- Score

32. Do we know what we need to know about this topic?
<--- Score

33. How does it fit into our organizational needs and tasks?
<--- Score

34. What does Virtual Desktop Infrastructure Monitoring success mean to the stakeholders?
<--- Score

35. How are the Virtual Desktop Infrastructure Monitoring's objectives aligned to the organization's overall business strategy?
<--- Score

36. What prevents me from making the changes I know will make me a more effective Virtual Desktop Infrastructure Monitoring leader?
<--- Score

37. How much are sponsors, customers, partners, stakeholders involved in Virtual Desktop Infrastructure Monitoring? In other words, what are the risks, if Virtual Desktop Infrastructure Monitoring does not deliver successfully?
<--- Score

38. When a Virtual Desktop Infrastructure Monitoring manager recognizes a problem, what options are available?
<--- Score

39. As a sponsor, customer or management, how important is it to meet goals, objectives?
<--- Score

40. Will Virtual Desktop Infrastructure Monitoring deliverables need to be tested and, if so, by whom?
<--- Score

41. Will new equipment/products be required to facilitate Virtual Desktop Infrastructure Monitoring delivery for example is new software needed?
<--- Score

42. What would happen if Virtual Desktop Infrastructure Monitoring weren't done?
<--- Score

43. What else needs to be measured?
<--- Score

44. What training and capacity building actions are needed to implement proposed reforms?
<--- Score

45. Will a response program recognize when a crisis occurs and provide some level of response?
<--- Score

46. Are controls defined to recognize and contain problems?
<--- Score

47. For your Virtual Desktop Infrastructure Monitoring project, identify and describe the business environment. is there more than one layer to the business environment?
<--- Score

Add up total points for this section:
_ _ _ _ _ = Total points for this section

Divided by: _ _ _ _ _ _ (number of statements answered) = _ _ _ _ _ _
Average score for this section

Transfer your score to the Virtual Desktop Infrastructure Monitoring Index at the beginning of the Self-Assessment.

CRITERION #2: DEFINE:

INTENT: Formulate the business problem. Define the problem, needs and objectives.

In my belief, the answer to this question is clearly defined:

5 Strongly Agree

4 Agree

3 Neutral

2 Disagree

1 Strongly Disagree

1. When was the Virtual Desktop Infrastructure Monitoring start date?
<--- Score

2. What is the minimum educational requirement for potential new hires?
<--- Score

3. How would you define the culture here?

<--- Score

4. What are the compelling business reasons
for embarking on Virtual Desktop Infrastructure
Monitoring?
<--- Score

5. Is there regularly 100% attendance at the team
meetings? If not, have appointed substitutes
attended to preserve cross-functionality and full
representation?
<--- Score

6. Has a high-level 'as is' process map been completed,
verified and validated?
<--- Score

7. Have all of the relationships been defined properly?
<--- Score

8. Is the Virtual Desktop Infrastructure Monitoring
scope manageable?
<--- Score

9. Are team charters developed?
<--- Score

10. Is the team formed and are team leaders (Coaches
and Management Leads) assigned?
<--- Score

11. How did the Virtual Desktop Infrastructure
Monitoring manager receive input to the
development of a Virtual Desktop Infrastructure
Monitoring improvement plan and the estimated
completion dates/times of each activity?

<--- Score

12. Is Virtual Desktop Infrastructure Monitoring currently on schedule according to the plan?
<--- Score

13. What are the Roles and Responsibilities for each team member and its leadership? Where is this documented?
<--- Score

14. How would one define Virtual Desktop Infrastructure Monitoring leadership?
<--- Score

15. Are different versions of process maps needed to account for the different types of inputs?
<--- Score

16. Is full participation by members in regularly held team meetings guaranteed?
<--- Score

17. Is the team equipped with available and reliable resources?
<--- Score

18. In what way can we redefine the criteria of choice in our category in our favor, as Method introduced style and design to cleaning and Virgin America returned glamor to flying?
<--- Score

19. Are business processes mapped?
<--- Score

20. Is there a Virtual Desktop Infrastructure Monitoring management charter, including business case, problem and goal statements, scope, milestones, roles and responsibilities, communication plan?
<--- Score

21. Do we all define Virtual Desktop Infrastructure Monitoring in the same way?
<--- Score

22. How will variation in the actual durations of each activity be dealt with to ensure that the expected Virtual Desktop Infrastructure Monitoring results are met?
<--- Score

23. Has anyone else (internal or external to the organization) attempted to solve this problem or a similar one before? If so, what knowledge can be leveraged from these previous efforts?
<--- Score

24. Is the improvement team aware of the different versions of a process: what they think it is vs. what it actually is vs. what it should be vs. what it could be?
<--- Score

25. Has the improvement team collected the 'voice of the customer' (obtained feedback – qualitative and quantitative)?
<--- Score

26. Is there a completed, verified, and validated high-level 'as is' (not 'should be' or 'could be') business process map?
<--- Score

27. Has/have the customer(s) been identified?
<--- Score

28. Will team members perform Virtual Desktop Infrastructure Monitoring work when assigned and in a timely fashion?
<--- Score

29. Has a team charter been developed and communicated?
<--- Score

30. Does the team have regular meetings?
<--- Score

31. Has the Virtual Desktop Infrastructure Monitoring work been fairly and/or equitably divided and delegated among team members who are qualified and capable to perform the work? Has everyone contributed?
<--- Score

32. Are task requirements clearly defined?
<--- Score

33. Is there a completed SIPOC representation, describing the Suppliers, Inputs, Process, Outputs, and Customers?
<--- Score

34. What would be the goal or target for a Virtual Desktop Infrastructure Monitoring's improvement team?
<--- Score

35. Has the direction changed at all during the course of Virtual Desktop Infrastructure Monitoring? If so, when did it change and why?
<--- Score

36. Is there a critical path to deliver Virtual Desktop Infrastructure Monitoring results?
<--- Score

37. Are customer(s) identified and segmented according to their different needs and requirements?
<--- Score

38. How will the Virtual Desktop Infrastructure Monitoring team and the organization measure complete success of Virtual Desktop Infrastructure Monitoring?
<--- Score

39. If substitutes have been appointed, have they been briefed on the Virtual Desktop Infrastructure Monitoring goals and received regular communications as to the progress to date?
<--- Score

40. Are audit criteria, scope, frequency and methods defined?
<--- Score

41. Who defines (or who defined) the rules and roles?
<--- Score

42. Is the team adequately staffed with the desired cross-functionality? If not, what additional resources are available to the team?
<--- Score

43. How and when will the baselines be defined?
<--- Score

44. Are roles and responsibilities formally defined?
<--- Score

45. What defines Best in Class?
<--- Score

46. How can the value of Virtual Desktop Infrastructure Monitoring be defined?
<--- Score

47. How does the Virtual Desktop Infrastructure Monitoring manager ensure against scope creep?
<--- Score

48. Are there different segments of customers?
<--- Score

49. Are accountability and ownership for Virtual Desktop Infrastructure Monitoring clearly defined?
<--- Score

50. Has a project plan, Gantt chart, or similar been developed/completed?
<--- Score

51. When is the estimated completion date?
<--- Score

52. What are the boundaries of the scope? What is in bounds and what is not? What is the start point? What is the stop point?
<--- Score

53. Are there any constraints known that bear on the ability to perform Virtual Desktop Infrastructure Monitoring work? How is the team addressing them?
<--- Score

54. How is the team tracking and documenting its work?
<--- Score

55. Is the scope of Virtual Desktop Infrastructure Monitoring defined?
<--- Score

56. When are meeting minutes sent out? Who is on the distribution list?
<--- Score

57. What constraints exist that might impact the team?
<--- Score

58. Will team members regularly document their Virtual Desktop Infrastructure Monitoring work?
<--- Score

59. Is Virtual Desktop Infrastructure Monitoring linked to key business goals and objectives?
<--- Score

60. In what way can we redefine the criteria of choice clients have in our category in our favor?
<--- Score

61. Are improvement team members fully trained on Virtual Desktop Infrastructure Monitoring?

<--- Score

62. What baselines are required to be defined and managed?
<--- Score

63. Is the current 'as is' process being followed? If not, what are the discrepancies?
<--- Score

64. Is data collected and displayed to better understand customer(s) critical needs and requirements.
<--- Score

65. Are customers identified and high impact areas defined?
<--- Score

66. How often are the team meetings?
<--- Score

67. What key business process output measure(s) does Virtual Desktop Infrastructure Monitoring leverage and how?
<--- Score

68. Have specific policy objectives been defined?
<--- Score

69. Is a fully trained team formed, supported, and committed to work on the Virtual Desktop Infrastructure Monitoring improvements?
<--- Score

70. What are the rough order estimates on cost

savings/opportunities that Virtual Desktop Infrastructure Monitoring brings?

<--- Score

71. Who are the Virtual Desktop Infrastructure Monitoring improvement team members, including Management Leads and Coaches?

<--- Score

72. Is it clearly defined in and to your organization what you do?

<--- Score

73. What critical content must be communicated – who, what, when, where, and how?

<--- Score

74. How do you keep key subject matter experts in the loop?

<--- Score

75. What are the dynamics of the communication plan?

<--- Score

76. Is the team sponsored by a champion or business leader?

<--- Score

77. How was the 'as is' process map developed, reviewed, verified and validated?

<--- Score

78. Have all basic functions of Virtual Desktop Infrastructure Monitoring been defined?

<--- Score

79. Are approval levels defined for contracts and supplements to contracts?
<--- Score

80. Is Virtual Desktop Infrastructure Monitoring Required?
<--- Score

81. Do the problem and goal statements meet the SMART criteria (specific, measurable, attainable, relevant, and time-bound)?
<--- Score

82. What specifically is the problem? Where does it occur? When does it occur? What is its extent?
<--- Score

83. Are Required Metrics Defined?
<--- Score

84. What customer feedback methods were used to solicit their input?
<--- Score

85. Have the customer needs been translated into specific, measurable requirements? How?
<--- Score

86. Has everyone on the team, including the team leaders, been properly trained?
<--- Score

Add up total points for this section:
_ _ _ _ _ = Total points for this section

Divided by: _____ (number of
statements answered) = _____
Average score for this section

Transfer your score to the Virtual
Desktop Infrastructure Monitoring
Index at the beginning of the Self-
Assessment.

CRITERION #3: MEASURE:

INTENT: Gather the correct data.
Measure the current performance and
evolution of the situation.

In my belief, the answer to this
question is clearly defined:

5 Strongly Agree

4 Agree

3 Neutral

2 Disagree

1 Strongly Disagree

1. What are the key input variables? What are the key process variables? What are the key output variables?
<--- Score

2. How do we do risk analysis of rare, cascading, catastrophic events?
<--- Score

3. What about Virtual Desktop Infrastructure

Monitoring Analysis of results?
<--- Score

4. Are key measures identified and agreed upon?
<--- Score

5. Who should receive measurement reports ?
<--- Score

6. Is the solution cost-effective?
<--- Score

7. Customer Measures: How Do Customers See Us?
<--- Score

8. Among the Virtual Desktop Infrastructure Monitoring product and service cost to be estimated, which is considered hardest to estimate?
<--- Score

9. Is this an issue for analysis or intuition?
<--- Score

10. Which customers can't participate in our market because they lack skills, wealth, or convenient access to existing solutions?
<--- Score

11. What is measured?
<--- Score

12. What are the uncertainties surrounding estimates of impact?
<--- Score

13. How frequently do you track Virtual Desktop Infrastructure Monitoring measures?
<--- Score

14. What measurements are possible, practicable and meaningful?
<--- Score

15. Have you found any 'ground fruit' or 'low-hanging fruit' for immediate remedies to the gap in performance?
<--- Score

16. How can you measure Virtual Desktop Infrastructure Monitoring in a systematic way?
<--- Score

17. Are high impact defects defined and identified in the business process?
<--- Score

18. How frequently do we track measures?
<--- Score

19. Is key measure data collection planned and executed, process variation displayed and communicated and performance baselined?
<--- Score

20. Does the Virtual Desktop Infrastructure Monitoring task fit the client's priorities?
<--- Score

21. Is data collection planned and executed?
<--- Score

22. How is Knowledge Management Measured?
<--- Score

23. What are the costs of reform?
<--- Score

24. What key measures identified indicate the performance of the business process?
<--- Score

25. Are the units of measure consistent?
<--- Score

26. Have all non-recommended alternatives been analyzed in sufficient detail?
<--- Score

27. Where is it measured?
<--- Score

28. Is long term and short term variability accounted for?
<--- Score

29. Why Measure?
<--- Score

30. Is data collected on key measures that were identified?
<--- Score

31. What charts has the team used to display the components of variation in the process?
<--- Score

32. Does Virtual Desktop Infrastructure

Monitoring analysis show the relationships among important Virtual Desktop Infrastructure Monitoring factors?

<--- Score

33. Does Virtual Desktop Infrastructure Monitoring analysis isolate the fundamental causes of problems?

<--- Score

34. Meeting the challenge: are missed Virtual Desktop Infrastructure Monitoring opportunities costing us money?

<--- Score

35. How to measure lifecycle phases?

<--- Score

36. How large is the gap between current performance and the customer-specified (goal) performance?

<--- Score

37. Who participated in the data collection for measurements?

<--- Score

38. How is the value delivered by Virtual Desktop Infrastructure Monitoring being measured?

<--- Score

39. What are the agreed upon definitions of the high impact areas, defect(s), unit(s), and opportunities that will figure into the process capability metrics?

<--- Score

40. Have changes been properly/adequately analyzed for effect?
<--- Score

41. What are your key Virtual Desktop Infrastructure Monitoring organizational performance measures, including key short and longer-term financial measures?
<--- Score

42. Will Virtual Desktop Infrastructure Monitoring have an impact on current business continuity, disaster recovery processes and/or infrastructure?
<--- Score

43. Can we do Virtual Desktop Infrastructure Monitoring without complex (expensive) analysis?
<--- Score

44. Why identify and analyze stakeholders and their interests?
<--- Score

45. Why do the measurements/indicators matter?
<--- Score

46. What potential environmental factors impact the Virtual Desktop Infrastructure Monitoring effort?
<--- Score

47. What is the right balance of time and resources between investigation, analysis, and discussion and dissemination?
<--- Score

48. Are you taking your company in the direction of better and revenue or cheaper and cost?
<--- Score

49. What particular quality tools did the team find helpful in establishing measurements?
<--- Score

50. What are my customers expectations and measures?
<--- Score

51. What measurements are being captured?
<--- Score

52. How will your organization measure success?
<--- Score

53. The approach of traditional Virtual Desktop Infrastructure Monitoring works for detail complexity but is focused on a systematic approach rather than an understanding of the nature of systems themselves. what approach will permit us to deal with the kind of unpredictable emergent behaviors that dynamic complexity can introduce?
<--- Score

54. Is Process Variation Displayed/Communicated?
<--- Score

55. What will be measured?
<--- Score

56. Will We Aggregate Measures across Priorities?
<--- Score

57. Schedule Development, Feasibility Analysis, Virtual Desktop Infrastructure Monitoring Management, Project Closings, Technique: Using the Critical Path Method
<--- Score

58. What methods are feasible and acceptable to estimate the impact of reforms?
<--- Score

59. Is performance measured?
<--- Score

60. Does the practice systematically track and analyze outcomes related for accountability and quality improvement?
<--- Score

61. What to measure and why?
<--- Score

62. What is the total cost related to deploying Virtual Desktop Infrastructure Monitoring, including any consulting or professional services?
<--- Score

63. How can we measure the performance?
<--- Score

64. How will effects be measured?
<--- Score

65. Are process variation components displayed/communicated using suitable charts, graphs, plots?
<--- Score

66. Do we aggressively reward and promote the people who have the biggest impact on creating excellent Virtual Desktop Infrastructure Monitoring services/products?
<--- Score

67. Are we taking our company in the direction of better and revenue or cheaper and cost?
<--- Score

68. Which customers cant participate in our Virtual Desktop Infrastructure Monitoring domain because they lack skills, wealth, or convenient access to existing solutions?
<--- Score

69. Are there any easy-to-implement alternatives to Virtual Desktop Infrastructure Monitoring? Sometimes other solutions are available that do not require the cost implications of a full-blown project?
<--- Score

70. Why should we expend time and effort to implement measurement?
<--- Score

71. How do you identify and analyze stakeholders and their interests?
<--- Score

72. Are the measurements objective?
<--- Score

73. What are the types and number of measures to use?

<--- Score

74. Which Stakeholder Characteristics Are Analyzed?
<--- Score

75. How will you measure your Virtual Desktop
Infrastructure Monitoring effectiveness?
<--- Score

76. Can We Measure the Return on Analysis?
<--- Score

77. What evidence is there and what is measured?
<--- Score

**78. How do your measurements capture
actionable Virtual Desktop Infrastructure
Monitoring information for use in exceeding
your customers expectations and securing your
customers engagement?**
<--- Score

79. How is progress measured?
<--- Score

80. Does Virtual Desktop Infrastructure Monitoring
systematically track and analyze outcomes for
accountability and quality improvement?
<--- Score

81. What has the team done to assure the stability and
accuracy of the measurement process?
<--- Score

82. What is an unallowable cost?
<--- Score

83. What Relevant Entities could be measured?
<--- Score

84. Is a solid data collection plan established that includes measurement systems analysis?
<--- Score

85. Do we effectively measure and reward individual and team performance?
<--- Score

86. How are measurements made?
<--- Score

87. Is there a Performance Baseline?
<--- Score

88. Is it possible to estimate the impact of unanticipated complexity such as wrong or failed assumptions, feedback, etc. on proposed reforms?
<--- Score

89. Have the types of risks that may impact Virtual Desktop Infrastructure Monitoring been identified and analyzed?
<--- Score

90. Was a data collection plan established?
<--- Score

91. How Will We Measure Success?
<--- Score

92. Why do measure/indicators matter?
<--- Score

93. What are our key indicators that you will measure, analyze and track?
<--- Score

94. Have the concerns of stakeholders to help identify and define potential barriers been obtained and analyzed?
<--- Score

95. Do staff have the necessary skills to collect, analyze, and report data?
<--- Score

96. How are you going to measure success?
<--- Score

97. How do you measure success?
<--- Score

98. What should be measured?
<--- Score

99. Are there measurements based on task performance?
<--- Score

100. How to measure variability?
<--- Score

101. How will success or failure be measured?
<--- Score

102. Are losses documented, analyzed, and remedial processes developed to prevent future losses?
<--- Score

103. What data was collected (past, present, future/ongoing)?
<--- Score

104. When is Knowledge Management Measured?
<--- Score

105. How do we focus on what is right -not who is right?
<--- Score

106. What are measures?
<--- Score

107. How will measures be used to manage and adapt?
<--- Score

Add up total points for this section:
_ _ _ _ _ = Total points for this section

Divided by: _ _ _ _ _ _ (number of statements answered) = _ _ _ _ _ _
Average score for this section

Transfer your score to the Virtual Desktop Infrastructure Monitoring Index at the beginning of the Self-Assessment.

CRITERION #4: ANALYZE:

INTENT: Analyze causes, assumptions
and hypotheses.

In my belief, the answer to this
question is clearly defined:

5 Strongly Agree

4 Agree

3 Neutral

2 Disagree

1 Strongly Disagree

1. What are the best opportunities for value
improvement?
<--- Score

2. Was a cause-and-effect diagram used to explore the
different types of causes (or sources of variation)?
<--- Score

3. Where is the data coming from to measure
compliance?

<--- Score

4. Was a detailed process map created to amplify critical steps of the 'as is' business process?
<--- Score

5. What quality tools were used to get through the analyze phase?
<--- Score

6. Is the Virtual Desktop Infrastructure Monitoring process severely broken such that a re-design is necessary?
<--- Score

7. How do you use Virtual Desktop Infrastructure Monitoring data and information to support organizational decision making and innovation?
<--- Score

8. When conducting a business process reengineering study, what should we look for when trying to identify business processes to change?
<--- Score

9. Are gaps between current performance and the goal performance identified?
<--- Score

10. Is the gap/opportunity displayed and communicated in financial terms?
<--- Score

11. Teaches and consults on quality process improvement, project management, and accelerated

Virtual Desktop Infrastructure Monitoring techniques
<--- Score

12. What other organizational variables, such as reward systems or communication systems, affect the performance of this Virtual Desktop Infrastructure Monitoring process?
<--- Score

13. What were the crucial 'moments of truth' on the process map?
<--- Score

14. An organizationally feasible system request is one that considers the mission, goals and objectives of the organization. key questions are: is the solution request practical and will it solve a problem or take advantage of an opportunity to achieve company goals?
<--- Score

15. Have the problem and goal statements been updated to reflect the additional knowledge gained from the analyze phase?
<--- Score

16. How often will data be collected for measures?
<--- Score

17. What were the financial benefits resulting from any 'ground fruit or low-hanging fruit' (quick fixes)?
<--- Score

18. What are the revised rough estimates of the financial savings/opportunity for Virtual Desktop Infrastructure Monitoring improvements?

<--- Score

19. How do mission and objectives affect the Virtual Desktop Infrastructure Monitoring processes of our organization?
<--- Score

20. What does the data say about the performance of the business process?
<--- Score

21. Do our leaders quickly bounce back from setbacks?
<--- Score

22. What successful thing are we doing today that may be blinding us to new growth opportunities?
<--- Score

23. What process should we select for improvement?
<--- Score

24. How do you measure the Operational performance of your key work systems and processes, including productivity, cycle time, and other appropriate measures of process effectiveness, efficiency, and innovation?
<--- Score

25. What did the team gain from developing a sub-process map?
<--- Score

26. What conclusions were drawn from the team's data collection and analysis? How did the team reach these conclusions?

<--- Score

27. Is the suppliers process defined and controlled?
<--- Score

28. Were Pareto charts (or similar) used to portray the 'heavy hitters' (or key sources of variation)?
<--- Score

29. Record-keeping requirements flow from the records needed as inputs, outputs, controls and for transformation of a Virtual Desktop Infrastructure Monitoring process. ask yourself: are the records needed as inputs to the Virtual Desktop Infrastructure Monitoring process available?
<--- Score

30. What is the cost of poor quality as supported by the team's analysis?
<--- Score

31. What tools were used to generate the list of possible causes?
<--- Score

32. How does the organization define, manage, and improve its Virtual Desktop Infrastructure Monitoring processes?
<--- Score

33. What are our Virtual Desktop Infrastructure Monitoring Processes?
<--- Score

34. A compounding model resolution with

available relevant data can often provide insight towards a solution methodology; which Virtual Desktop Infrastructure Monitoring models, tools and techniques are necessary?
<--- Score

35. What are the disruptive Virtual Desktop Infrastructure Monitoring technologies that enable our organization to radically change our business processes?
<--- Score

36. What are your current levels and trends in key measures or indicators of Virtual Desktop Infrastructure Monitoring product and process performance that are important to and directly serve your customers? how do these results compare with the performance of your competitors and other organizations with similar offerings?
<--- Score

37. Think about some of the processes you undertake within your organization. which do you own?
<--- Score

38. Were there any improvement opportunities identified from the process analysis?
<--- Score

39. Do your employees have the opportunity to do what they do best everyday?
<--- Score

40. Is the performance gap determined?

<--- Score

41. Is Data and process analysis, root cause analysis and quantifying the gap/opportunity in place?
<--- Score

42. What controls do we have in place to protect data?
<--- Score

43. Have any additional benefits been identified that will result from closing all or most of the gaps?
<--- Score

44. Did any value-added analysis or 'lean thinking' take place to identify some of the gaps shown on the 'as is' process map?
<--- Score

45. How is the way you as the leader think and process information affecting your organizational culture?
<--- Score

46. What are your current levels and trends in key Virtual Desktop Infrastructure Monitoring measures or indicators of product and process performance that are important to and directly serve your customers?
<--- Score

47. Do you, as a leader, bounce back quickly from setbacks?
<--- Score

48. Identify an operational issue in your organization. for example, could a particular task be done more quickly or more efficiently?

<--- Score

49. Think about the functions involved in your Virtual Desktop Infrastructure Monitoring project. what processes flow from these functions?
<--- Score

50. What tools were used to narrow the list of possible causes?
<--- Score

51. How was the detailed process map generated, verified, and validated?
<--- Score

52. Did any additional data need to be collected?
<--- Score

53. Can we add value to the current Virtual Desktop Infrastructure Monitoring decision-making process (largely qualitative) by incorporating uncertainty modeling (more quantitative)?
<--- Score

54. How do we promote understanding that opportunity for improvement is not criticism of the status quo, or the people who created the status quo?
<--- Score

55. Were any designed experiments used to generate additional insight into the data analysis?
<--- Score

56. What other jobs or tasks affect the

performance of the steps in the Virtual Desktop Infrastructure Monitoring process?
<--- Score

Add up total points for this section:
_ _ _ _ _ = Total points for this section

Divided by: _ _ _ _ _ _ (number of statements answered) = _ _ _ _ _ _
Average score for this section

Transfer your score to the Virtual Desktop Infrastructure Monitoring Index at the beginning of the Self-Assessment.

CRITERION #5: IMPROVE:

INTENT: Develop a practical solution.
Innovate, establish and test the
solution and to measure the results.

In my belief, the answer to this
question is clearly defined:

5 Strongly Agree

4 Agree

3 Neutral

2 Disagree

1 Strongly Disagree

1. Is there a cost/benefit analysis of optimal
solution(s)?
<--- Score

2. How will you know when its improved?
<--- Score

**3. How do we decide how much to remunerate an
employee?**

<--- Score

4. If you could go back in time five years, what decision would you make differently? What is your best guess as to what decision you're making today you might regret five years from now?
<--- Score

5. Who controls key decisions that will be made?
<--- Score

6. How do we measure improved Virtual Desktop Infrastructure Monitoring service perception, and satisfaction?
<--- Score

7. Is the measure understandable to a variety of people?
<--- Score

8. What can we do to improve?
<--- Score

9. How will you measure the results?
<--- Score

10. How do the Virtual Desktop Infrastructure Monitoring results compare with the performance of your competitors and other organizations with similar offerings?
<--- Score

11. Is a contingency plan established?
<--- Score

12. Is the optimal solution selected based on testing

and analysis?
<--- Score

13. What is the magnitude of the improvements?
<--- Score

14. How do we Improve Virtual Desktop Infrastructure Monitoring service perception, and satisfaction?
<--- Score

15. What tools were most useful during the improve phase?
<--- Score

16. How do you improve your likelihood of success ?
<--- Score

17. What actually has to improve and by how much?
<--- Score

18. How can we improve Virtual Desktop Infrastructure Monitoring?
<--- Score

19. What evaluation strategy is needed and what needs to be done to assure its implementation and use?
<--- Score

20. What is the Virtual Desktop Infrastructure Monitoring sustainability risk?
<--- Score

21. How does the team improve its work?
<--- Score

22. Explorations of the frontiers of Virtual Desktop Infrastructure Monitoring will help you build influence, improve Virtual Desktop Infrastructure Monitoring, optimize decision making, and sustain change
<--- Score

23. What are the implications of this decision 10 minutes, 10 months, and 10 years from now?
<--- Score

24. Who will be using the results of the measurement activities?
<--- Score

25. What were the underlying assumptions on the cost-benefit analysis?
<--- Score

26. What lessons, if any, from a pilot were incorporated into the design of the full-scale solution?
<--- Score

27. Is there a small-scale pilot for proposed improvement(s)? What conclusions were drawn from the outcomes of a pilot?
<--- Score

28. Who controls the risk?
<--- Score

29. Were any criteria developed to assist the team in testing and evaluating potential solutions?
<--- Score

30. How to Improve?
<--- Score

31. How can we improve performance?
<--- Score

32. What went well, what should change, what can improve?
<--- Score

33. What do we want to improve?
<--- Score

34. Is the implementation plan designed?
<--- Score

35. What improvements have been achieved?
<--- Score

36. Are possible solutions generated and tested?
<--- Score

37. Does the goal represent a desired result that can be measured?
<--- Score

38. Are there any constraints (technical, political, cultural, or otherwise) that would inhibit certain solutions?
<--- Score

39. What tools do you use once you have decided on a Virtual Desktop Infrastructure Monitoring strategy and more importantly how do you choose?
<--- Score

40. How do you measure progress and evaluate training effectiveness?
<--- Score

41. What tools were used to tap into the creativity and encourage 'outside the box' thinking?
<--- Score

42. What is the implementation plan?
<--- Score

43. What needs improvement?
<--- Score

44. How do we measure risk?
<--- Score

45. For estimation problems, how do you develop an estimation statement?
<--- Score

46. How did the team generate the list of possible solutions?
<--- Score

47. Is pilot data collected and analyzed?
<--- Score

48. Are we using Virtual Desktop Infrastructure Monitoring to communicate information about our Cybersecurity Risk Management programs including the effectiveness of those programs to stakeholders, including boards, investors, auditors, and insurers?
<--- Score

49. Is there a high likelihood that any recommendations will achieve their intended results?

<--- Score

50. Are we Assessing Virtual Desktop Infrastructure Monitoring and Risk?

<--- Score

51. How significant is the improvement in the eyes of the end user?

<--- Score

52. How will the team or the process owner(s) monitor the implementation plan to see that it is working as intended?

<--- Score

53. How do we keep improving Virtual Desktop Infrastructure Monitoring?

<--- Score

54. Is a solution implementation plan established, including schedule/work breakdown structure, resources, risk management plan, cost/budget, and control plan?

<--- Score

55. What communications are necessary to support the implementation of the solution?

<--- Score

56. At what point will vulnerability assessments be performed once Virtual Desktop Infrastructure Monitoring is put into production (e.g., ongoing

Risk Management after implementation)?
<--- Score

57. Risk factors: what are the characteristics of Virtual Desktop Infrastructure Monitoring that make it risky?
<--- Score

58. Do we cover the five essential competencies-Communication, Collaboration,Innovation, Adaptability, and Leadership that improve an organization's ability to leverage the new Virtual Desktop Infrastructure Monitoring in a volatile global economy?
<--- Score

59. For decision problems, how do you develop a decision statement?
<--- Score

60. Are improved process ('should be') maps modified based on pilot data and analysis?
<--- Score

61. What does the 'should be' process map/design look like?
<--- Score

62. What is the team's contingency plan for potential problems occurring in implementation?
<--- Score

63. How will you know that you have improved?
<--- Score

64. Who will be responsible for making the decisions

to include or exclude requested changes once Virtual Desktop Infrastructure Monitoring is underway?
<--- Score

65. To what extent does management recognize Virtual Desktop Infrastructure Monitoring as a tool to increase the results?
<--- Score

66. How can skill-level changes improve Virtual Desktop Infrastructure Monitoring?
<--- Score

67. How will the organization know that the solution worked?
<--- Score

68. What is the risk?
<--- Score

69. How will we know that a change is improvement?
<--- Score

70. Was a pilot designed for the proposed solution(s)?
<--- Score

71. Are new and improved process ('should be') maps developed?
<--- Score

72. How do we go about Comparing Virtual Desktop Infrastructure Monitoring approaches/solutions?
<--- Score

73. Risk events: what are the things that could go wrong?

<--- Score

74. What to do with the results or outcomes of measurements?
<--- Score

75. How important is the completion of a recognized college or graduate-level degree program in the hiring decision?
<--- Score

76. What attendant changes will need to be made to ensure that the solution is successful?
<--- Score

77. Are the best solutions selected?
<--- Score

78. Do we combine technical expertise with business knowledge and Virtual Desktop Infrastructure Monitoring Key topics include lifecycles, development approaches, requirements and how to make a business case?
<--- Score

79. How do we improve productivity?
<--- Score

80. Who are the people involved in developing and implementing Virtual Desktop Infrastructure Monitoring?
<--- Score

81. What resources are required for the improvement effort?
<--- Score

82. How Do We Link Measurement and Risk?
<--- Score

83. Why improve in the first place?
<--- Score

84. What error proofing will be done to address some of the discrepancies observed in the 'as is' process?
<--- Score

85. Can the solution be designed and implemented within an acceptable time period?
<--- Score

86. What tools were used to evaluate the potential solutions?
<--- Score

87. How does the solution remove the key sources of issues discovered in the analyze phase?
<--- Score

88. In the past few months, what is the smallest change we have made that has had the biggest positive result? What was it about that small change that produced the large return?
<--- Score

89. What should a proof of concept or pilot accomplish?
<--- Score

90. Describe the design of the pilot and what tests were conducted, if any?
<--- Score

91. Who will be responsible for documenting the Virtual Desktop Infrastructure Monitoring requirements in detail?

<--- Score

92. What is Virtual Desktop Infrastructure Monitoring's impact on utilizing the best solution(s)?

<--- Score

93. Is the solution technically practical?

<--- Score

94. Is Supporting Virtual Desktop Infrastructure Monitoring documentation required?

<--- Score

95. How do you manage and improve your Virtual Desktop Infrastructure Monitoring work systems to deliver customer value and achieve organizational success and sustainability?

<--- Score

Add up total points for this section:

_ _ _ _ _ = Total points for this section

Divided by: _ _ _ _ _ _ (number of statements answered) = _ _ _ _ _ _ Average score for this section

Transfer your score to the Virtual Desktop Infrastructure Monitoring Index at the beginning of the Self-Assessment.

CRITERION #6: CONTROL:

INTENT: Implement the practical solution. Maintain the performance and correct possible complications.

In my belief, the answer to this question is clearly defined:

5 Strongly Agree

4 Agree

3 Neutral

2 Disagree

1 Strongly Disagree

1. Is there documentation that will support the successful operation of the improvement?
<--- Score

2. How will the process owner verify improvement in present and future sigma levels, process capabilities?
<--- Score

3. Are pertinent alerts monitored, analyzed and

distributed to appropriate personnel?

<--- Score

4. What are your results for key measures or indicators of the accomplishment of your Virtual Desktop Infrastructure Monitoring strategy and action plans, including building and strengthening core competencies?

<--- Score

5. How likely is the current Virtual Desktop Infrastructure Monitoring plan to come in on schedule or on budget?

<--- Score

6. Measure, Monitor and Predict Virtual Desktop Infrastructure Monitoring Activities to Optimize Operations and Profitably, and Enhance Outcomes

<--- Score

7. Is there a recommended audit plan for routine surveillance inspections of Virtual Desktop Infrastructure Monitoring's gains?

<--- Score

8. Will existing staff require re-training, for example, to learn new business processes?

<--- Score

9. Were the planned controls working?

<--- Score

10. What do we stand for--and what are we against?

<--- Score

11. How will the day-to-day responsibilities for monitoring and continual improvement be transferred from the improvement team to the process owner?
<--- Score

12. What are the critical parameters to watch?
<--- Score

13. Do you monitor the effectiveness of your Virtual Desktop Infrastructure Monitoring activities?
<--- Score

14. Is there a standardized process?
<--- Score

15. Implementation Planning- is a pilot needed to test the changes before a full roll out occurs?
<--- Score

16. Is a response plan established and deployed?
<--- Score

17. What can you control?
<--- Score

18. Is there a documented and implemented monitoring plan?
<--- Score

19. Does Virtual Desktop Infrastructure Monitoring appropriately measure and monitor risk?
<--- Score

20. What are we attempting to measure/monitor?

<--- Score

21. How will new or emerging customer needs/requirements be checked/communicated to orient the process toward meeting the new specifications and continually reducing variation?
<--- Score

22. Who will be in control?
<--- Score

23. How can we best use all of our knowledge repositories to enhance learning and sharing?
<--- Score

24. Will any special training be provided for results interpretation?
<--- Score

25. What should we measure to verify efficiency gains?
<--- Score

26. Who is the Virtual Desktop Infrastructure Monitoring process owner?
<--- Score

27. What key inputs and outputs are being measured on an ongoing basis?
<--- Score

28. Who controls critical resources?
<--- Score

29. Is knowledge gained on process shared and institutionalized?

<--- Score

30. How do our controls stack up?
<--- Score

31. What should we measure to verify effectiveness gains?
<--- Score

32. Does a troubleshooting guide exist or is it needed?
<--- Score

33. Against what alternative is success being measured?
<--- Score

34. Virtual Desktop Infrastructure Monitoring in management -Strategic planning
<--- Score

35. Does the response plan contain a definite closed loop continual improvement scheme (e.g., plan-do-check-act)?
<--- Score

36. How do you select, collect, align, and integrate Virtual Desktop Infrastructure Monitoring data and information for tracking daily operations and overall organizational performance, including progress relative to strategic objectives and action plans?
<--- Score

37. Whats the best design framework for Virtual Desktop Infrastructure Monitoring organization now that, in a post industrial-age if the top-down,

command and control model is no longer relevant?
<--- Score

38. How will the process owner and team be able to hold the gains?
<--- Score

39. Do we monitor the Virtual Desktop Infrastructure Monitoring decisions made and fine tune them as they evolve?
<--- Score

40. Were the planned controls in place?
<--- Score

41. Are documented procedures clear and easy to follow for the operators?
<--- Score

42. Does job training on the documented procedures need to be part of the process team's education and training?
<--- Score

43. Can Virtual Desktop Infrastructure Monitoring be learned?
<--- Score

44. Are suggested corrective/restorative actions indicated on the response plan for known causes to problems that might surface?
<--- Score

45. Are operating procedures consistent?
<--- Score

46. What should the next improvement project be that is related to Virtual Desktop Infrastructure Monitoring?

<--- Score

47. What are the key elements of your Virtual Desktop Infrastructure Monitoring performance improvement system, including your evaluation, organizational learning, and innovation processes?

<--- Score

48. What quality tools were useful in the control phase?

<--- Score

49. Is a response plan in place for when the input, process, or output measures indicate an 'out-of-control' condition?

<--- Score

50. What is the recommended frequency of auditing?

<--- Score

51. How will input, process, and output variables be checked to detect for sub-optimal conditions?

<--- Score

52. Are controls in place and consistently applied?

<--- Score

53. What other areas of the organization might benefit from the Virtual Desktop Infrastructure Monitoring team's improvements, knowledge, and learning?

<--- Score

54. Are new process steps, standards, and documentation ingrained into normal operations?
<--- Score

55. How do you encourage people to take control and responsibility?
<--- Score

56. What other systems, operations, processes, and infrastructures (hiring practices, staffing, training, incentives/rewards, metrics/dashboards/scorecards, etc.) need updates, additions, changes, or deletions in order to facilitate knowledge transfer and improvements?
<--- Score

57. Is there a Virtual Desktop Infrastructure Monitoring Communication plan covering who needs to get what information when?
<--- Score

58. What is the control/monitoring plan?
<--- Score

59. Is new knowledge gained imbedded in the response plan?
<--- Score

60. Has the improved process and its steps been standardized?
<--- Score

61. Is there a control plan in place for sustaining improvements (short and long-term)?
<--- Score

62. Do the Virtual Desktop Infrastructure Monitoring decisions we make today help people and the planet tomorrow?
<--- Score

63. In the case of a Virtual Desktop Infrastructure Monitoring project, the criteria for the audit derive from implementation objectives. an audit of a Virtual Desktop Infrastructure Monitoring project involves assessing whether the recommendations outlined for implementation have been met. Can we track that any Virtual Desktop Infrastructure Monitoring project is implemented as planned, and is it working?
<--- Score

64. Is there a transfer of ownership and knowledge to process owner and process team tasked with the responsibilities.
<--- Score

65. How might the organization capture best practices and lessons learned so as to leverage improvements across the business?
<--- Score

66. What are the known security controls?
<--- Score

67. Have new or revised work instructions resulted?
<--- Score

68. Do the decisions we make today help people and the planet tomorrow?
<--- Score

CRITERION #7: SUSTAIN:

INTENT: Retain the benefits.

In my belief, the answer to this question is clearly defined:

5 Strongly Agree

4 Agree

3 Neutral

2 Disagree

1 Strongly Disagree

1. What does your signature ensure?
<--- Score

2. If our customer were my grandmother, would I tell her to buy what we're selling?
<--- Score

3. What is it like to work for me?
<--- Score

4. How do we manage Virtual Desktop Infrastructure Monitoring Knowledge

Management (KM)?

<--- Score

5. Is it economical; do we have the time and money?

<--- Score

6. What is Tricky About This?

<--- Score

7. Is our strategy driving our strategy? Or is the way in which we allocate resources driving our strategy?

<--- Score

8. How can we become the company that would put us out of business?

<--- Score

9. Will I get fired?

<--- Score

10. To whom do you add value?

<--- Score

11. Do Virtual Desktop Infrastructure Monitoring rules make a reasonable demand on a users capabilities?

<--- Score

12. How much does Virtual Desktop Infrastructure Monitoring help?

<--- Score

13. Have benefits been optimized with all key stakeholders?

<--- Score

14. Who are the key stakeholders?
<--- Score

15. Is maximizing Virtual Desktop Infrastructure Monitoring protection the same as minimizing Virtual Desktop Infrastructure Monitoring loss?
<--- Score

16. What stupid rule would we most like to kill?
<--- Score

17. Who do we think the world wants us to be?
<--- Score

18. Who have we, as a company, historically been when we've been at our best?
<--- Score

19. How can we incorporate support to ensure safe and effective use of Virtual Desktop Infrastructure Monitoring into the services that we provide?
<--- Score

20. Are there Virtual Desktop Infrastructure Monitoring Models?
<--- Score

21. If you had to rebuild your organization without any traditional competitive advantages (i.e., no killer a technology, promising research, innovative product/service delivery model, etc.), how would your people have to approach their work and collaborate together in order to create the necessary conditions for success?
<--- Score

22. What is the overall business strategy?
<--- Score

23. How do we foster the skills, knowledge, talents, attributes, and characteristics we want to have?
<--- Score

24. What new services of functionality will be implemented next with Virtual Desktop Infrastructure Monitoring ?
<--- Score

25. What is the funding source for this project?
<--- Score

26. What are strategies for increasing support and reducing opposition?
<--- Score

27. What would I recommend my friend do if he were facing this dilemma?
<--- Score

28. We picked a method, now what?
<--- Score

29. How long will it take to change?
<--- Score

30. Do I know what I'm doing? And who do I call if I don't?
<--- Score

31. What are the short and long-term Virtual Desktop Infrastructure Monitoring goals?

<--- Score

32. How do we ensure that implementations of Virtual Desktop Infrastructure Monitoring products are done in a way that ensures safety?
<--- Score

33. What management system can we use to leverage the Virtual Desktop Infrastructure Monitoring experience, ideas, and concerns of the people closest to the work to be done?
<--- Score

34. Who will be responsible for deciding whether Virtual Desktop Infrastructure Monitoring goes ahead or not after the initial investigations?
<--- Score

35. How do you determine the key elements that affect Virtual Desktop Infrastructure Monitoring workforce satisfaction? how are these elements determined for different workforce groups and segments?
<--- Score

36. What are internal and external Virtual Desktop Infrastructure Monitoring relations?
<--- Score

37. What do we do when new problems arise?
<--- Score

38. Are we changing as fast as the world around us?
<--- Score

39. Do you have any supplemental information to

add to this checklist?
<--- Score

**40. What are the top 3 things at the forefront of
our Virtual Desktop Infrastructure Monitoring
agendas for the next 3 years?**
<--- Score

41. Did my employees make progress today?
<--- Score

42. Design Thinking: Integrating Innovation, Virtual
Desktop Infrastructure Monitoring Experience, and
Brand Value
<--- Score

43. Whom among your colleagues do you trust, and
for what?
<--- Score

**44. How do we engage the workforce, in addition
to satisfying them?**
<--- Score

**45. Do we think we know, or do we know we know
?**
<--- Score

46. Are we paying enough attention to the partners
our company depends on to succeed?
<--- Score

**47. Is there a limit on the number of users in
Virtual Desktop Infrastructure Monitoring ?**
<--- Score

48. Virtual Desktop Infrastructure Monitoring Service Sales Supply Chain, Procurement, Distribution
<--- Score

49. When information truly is ubiquitous, when reach and connectivity are completely global, when computing resources are infinite, and when a whole new set of impossibilities are not only possible, but happening, what will that do to our business?
<--- Score

50. Why should people listen to you?
<--- Score

51. If you were responsible for initiating and implementing major changes in your organization, what steps might you take to ensure acceptance of those changes?
<--- Score

52. How do senior leaders deploy your organizations vision and values through your leadership system, to the workforce, to key suppliers and partners, and to customers and other stakeholders, as appropriate?
<--- Score

53. Who is going to care?
<--- Score

54. How would our PR, marketing, and social media change if we did not use outside agencies?
<--- Score

55. Is Virtual Desktop Infrastructure Monitoring dependent on the successful delivery of a current

project?

<--- Score

56. How do we make it meaningful in connecting Virtual Desktop Infrastructure Monitoring with what users do day-to-day?

<--- Score

57. What counts that we are not counting?

<--- Score

58. Is the Virtual Desktop Infrastructure Monitoring organization completing tasks effectively and efficiently?

<--- Score

59. How Do We Know if We Are Successful?

<--- Score

60. What is your BATNA (best alternative to a negotiated agreement)?

<--- Score

61. What will be the consequences to the stakeholder (financial, reputation etc) if Virtual Desktop Infrastructure Monitoring does not go ahead or fails to deliver the objectives?

<--- Score

62. What are the long-term Virtual Desktop Infrastructure Monitoring goals?

<--- Score

63. Who do we want our customers to become?

<--- Score

64. How important is Virtual Desktop Infrastructure Monitoring to the user organizations mission?

<--- Score

65. How do we foster innovation?

<--- Score

66. Why don't our customers like us?

<--- Score

67. Are the criteria for selecting recommendations stated?

<--- Score

68. Where is our petri dish?

<--- Score

69. How will we know if we have been successful?

<--- Score

70. You may have created your customer policies at a time when you lacked resources, technology wasn't up-to-snuff, or low service levels were the industry norm. Have those circumstances changed?

<--- Score

71. What kind of crime could a potential new hire have committed that would not only not disqualify him/her from being hired by our organization, but would actually indicate that he/she might be a particularly good fit?

<--- Score

72. If we got kicked out and the board brought in a

new CEO, what would he do?

<--- Score

73. Will there be any necessary staff changes (redundancies or new hires)?

<--- Score

74. Marketing budgets are tighter, consumers are more skeptical, and social media has changed forever the way we talk about Virtual Desktop Infrastructure Monitoring. How do we gain traction?

<--- Score

75. Who is the main stakeholder, with ultimate responsibility for driving Virtual Desktop Infrastructure Monitoring forward?

<--- Score

76. In a project to restructure Virtual Desktop Infrastructure Monitoring outcomes, which stakeholders would you involve?

<--- Score

77. Who else should we help?

<--- Score

78. What is the range of capabilities?

<--- Score

79. Operational - will it work?

<--- Score

80. If we do not follow, then how to lead?

<--- Score

81. How do we go about Securing Virtual Desktop

Infrastructure Monitoring?
<--- Score

82. Who are four people whose careers I've enhanced?
<--- Score

83. Is the impact that Virtual Desktop Infrastructure Monitoring has shown?
<--- Score

84. Is a Virtual Desktop Infrastructure Monitoring Team Work effort in place?
<--- Score

85. Design Thinking: Integrating Innovation, Virtual Desktop Infrastructure Monitoring, and Brand Value
<--- Score

86. Do we say no to customers for no reason?
<--- Score

87. What knowledge, skills and characteristics mark a good Virtual Desktop Infrastructure Monitoring project manager?
<--- Score

88. If there were zero limitations, what would we do differently?
<--- Score

89. How will we ensure we get what we expected?
<--- Score

90. Are there any disadvantages to implementing Virtual Desktop Infrastructure Monitoring? There might be some that are less obvious?

<--- Score

91. What are the gaps in my knowledge and experience?
<--- Score

92. Do you see more potential in people than they do in themselves?
<--- Score

93. Among our stronger employees, how many see themselves at the company in three years? How many would leave for a 10 percent raise from another company?
<--- Score

94. Schedule -can it be done in the given time?
<--- Score

95. What is the estimated value of the project?
<--- Score

96. What are we challenging, in the sense that Mac challenged the PC or Dove tackled the Beauty Myth?
<--- Score

97. Who is On the Team?
<--- Score

98. Is there any reason to believe the opposite of my current belief?
<--- Score

99. What threat is Virtual Desktop Infrastructure Monitoring addressing?
<--- Score

100. What are specific Virtual Desktop Infrastructure Monitoring Rules to follow?
<--- Score

101. What was the last experiment we ran?
<--- Score

102. What are your most important goals for the strategic Virtual Desktop Infrastructure Monitoring objectives?
<--- Score

103. If I had to leave my organization for a year and the only communication I could have with employees was a single paragraph, what would I write?
<--- Score

104. Who are you going to put out of business, and why?
<--- Score

105. Do you keep 50% of your time unscheduled?
<--- Score

106. Why is it important to have senior management support for a Virtual Desktop Infrastructure Monitoring project?
<--- Score

107. Who, on the executive team or the board, has spoken to a customer recently?
<--- Score

108. What are all of our Virtual Desktop Infrastructure Monitoring domains and what do

they do?
<--- Score

109. How is business? Why?
<--- Score

110. Who will provide the final approval of Virtual Desktop Infrastructure Monitoring deliverables?
<--- Score

111. How to deal with Virtual Desktop Infrastructure Monitoring Changes?
<--- Score

112. Is there any existing Virtual Desktop Infrastructure Monitoring governance structure?
<--- Score

113. How will you know that the Virtual Desktop Infrastructure Monitoring project has been successful?
<--- Score

114. If we weren't already in this business, would we enter it today? And if not, what are we going to do about it?
<--- Score

115. What is Effective Virtual Desktop Infrastructure Monitoring?
<--- Score

116. What information is critical to our organization that our executives are ignoring?
<--- Score

117. How will we insure seamless interoperability of Virtual Desktop Infrastructure Monitoring moving forward?

<--- Score

118. How much contingency will be available in the budget?

<--- Score

119. What will drive Virtual Desktop Infrastructure Monitoring change?

<--- Score

120. Do we have enough freaky customers in our portfolio pushing us to the limit day in and day out?

<--- Score

121. How do we accomplish our long range Virtual Desktop Infrastructure Monitoring goals?

<--- Score

122. Your reputation and success is your lifeblood, and Virtual Desktop Infrastructure Monitoring shows you how to stay relevant, add value, and win and retain customers

<--- Score

123. Do you have an implicit bias for capital investments over people investments?

<--- Score

124. In what ways are Virtual Desktop Infrastructure Monitoring vendors and us interacting to ensure safe and effective use?

<--- Score

125. Do we have the right capabilities and capacities?

<--- Score

126. What would have to be true for the option on the table to be the best possible choice?

<--- Score

127. What are the challenges?

<--- Score

128. What am I trying to prove to myself, and how might it be hijacking my life and business success?

<--- Score

129. How can you negotiate Virtual Desktop Infrastructure Monitoring successfully with a stubborn boss, an irate client, or a deceitful coworker?

<--- Score

130. Can we maintain our growth without detracting from the factors that have contributed to our success?

<--- Score

131. Which criteria are used to determine which projects are going to be pursued or discarded?

<--- Score

132. Do we underestimate the customer's journey?

<--- Score

133. What are the rules and assumptions my industry operates under? What if the opposite were true?

<--- Score

134. Would you rather sell to knowledgeable and informed customers or to uninformed customers?
<--- Score

135. How likely is it that a customer would recommend our company to a friend or colleague?
<--- Score

136. Are new benefits received and understood?
<--- Score

137. Will it be accepted by users?
<--- Score

138. Have new benefits been realized?
<--- Score

139. What are the Key enablers to make this Virtual Desktop Infrastructure Monitoring move?
<--- Score

140. What is the purpose of Virtual Desktop Infrastructure Monitoring in relation to the mission?
<--- Score

141. If no one would ever find out about my accomplishments, how would I lead differently?
<--- Score

142. Are you satisfied with your current role? If not, what is missing from it?
<--- Score

143. How do we maintain Virtual Desktop Infrastructure Monitoring's Integrity?

<--- Score

144. Are we making progress? and are we making progress as Virtual Desktop Infrastructure Monitoring leaders?
<--- Score

145. Think about the kind of project structure that would be appropriate for your Virtual Desktop Infrastructure Monitoring project. should it be formal and complex, or can it be less formal and relatively simple?
<--- Score

146. Which individuals, teams or departments will be involved in Virtual Desktop Infrastructure Monitoring?
<--- Score

147. What are the usability implications of Virtual Desktop Infrastructure Monitoring actions?
<--- Score

148. Think of your Virtual Desktop Infrastructure Monitoring project. what are the main functions?
<--- Score

149. How are we doing compared to our industry?
<--- Score

150. What did we miss in the interview for the worst hire we ever made?
<--- Score

151. If our company went out of business tomorrow, would anyone who doesn't get a paycheck here care?
<--- Score

152. What trophy do we want on our mantle?
<--- Score

153. Why are Virtual Desktop Infrastructure Monitoring skills important?
<--- Score

154. Ask yourself: how would we do this work if we only had one staff member to do it?
<--- Score

155. Which models, tools and techniques are necessary?
<--- Score

156. Which functions and people interact with the supplier and or customer?
<--- Score

157. Where can we break convention?
<--- Score

158. How to Secure Virtual Desktop Infrastructure Monitoring?
<--- Score

159. Why should we adopt a Virtual Desktop Infrastructure Monitoring framework?
<--- Score

160. Are we / should we be Revolutionary or evolutionary?
<--- Score

161. Who Uses What?

<--- Score

162. Do you have a vision statement?
<--- Score

163. How does Virtual Desktop Infrastructure Monitoring integrate with other business initiatives?
<--- Score

164. What trouble can we get into?
<--- Score

165. What current systems have to be understood and/or changed?
<--- Score

166. In retrospect, of the projects that we pulled the plug on, what percent do we wish had been allowed to keep going, and what percent do we wish had ended earlier?
<--- Score

167. What sources do you use to gather information for a Virtual Desktop Infrastructure Monitoring study?
<--- Score

168. How do I stay inspired?
<--- Score

169. Who will manage the integration of tools?
<--- Score

170. What have we done to protect our business from competitive encroachment?
<--- Score

171. What are the business goals Virtual Desktop Infrastructure Monitoring is aiming to achieve?
<--- Score

172. What business benefits will Virtual Desktop Infrastructure Monitoring goals deliver if achieved?
<--- Score

173. What are the basics of Virtual Desktop Infrastructure Monitoring fraud?
<--- Score

174. Who uses our product in ways we never expected?
<--- Score

175. Are assumptions made in Virtual Desktop Infrastructure Monitoring stated explicitly?
<--- Score

176. Instead of going to current contacts for new ideas, what if you reconnected with dormant contacts--the people you used to know? If you were going reactivate a dormant tie, who would it be?
<--- Score

177. What is our Virtual Desktop Infrastructure Monitoring Strategy?
<--- Score

178. What one word do we want to own in the minds of our customers, employees, and partners?
<--- Score

179. Has implementation been effective in

reaching specified objectives?
<--- Score

180. How Do We Create Buy-in?
<--- Score

181. Am I failing differently each time?
<--- Score

182. What are the critical success factors?
<--- Score

183. How do we provide a safe environment -physically and emotionally?
<--- Score

184. What is our formula for success in Virtual Desktop Infrastructure Monitoring ?
<--- Score

185. What is a feasible sequencing of reform initiatives over time?
<--- Score

186. What is the craziest thing we can do?
<--- Score

187. What potential megatrends could make our business model obsolete?
<--- Score

188. Are the assumptions believable and achievable?
<--- Score

189. Were lessons learned captured and

communicated?
<--- Score

190. Which Virtual Desktop Infrastructure Monitoring goals are the most important?
<--- Score

191. What is the mission of the organization?
<--- Score

192. Do we have the right people on the bus?
<--- Score

193. How do we keep the momentum going?
<--- Score

194. Who is responsible for errors?
<--- Score

195. What is something you believe that nearly no one agrees with you on?
<--- Score

196. What happens at this company when people fail?
<--- Score

197. Who will determine interim and final deadlines?
<--- Score

198. In the past year, what have you done (or could you have done) to increase the accurate perception of this company/brand as ethical and honest?
<--- Score

199. How will we build a 100-year startup?

<--- Score

200. Political -is anyone trying to undermine this project?

<--- Score

201. Who will use it?

<--- Score

202. What should we stop doing?

<--- Score

203. What happens when a new employee joins the organization?

<--- Score

204. What happens if you do not have enough funding?

<--- Score

205. Are we relevant? Will we be relevant five years from now? Ten?

<--- Score

206. What is our competitive advantage?

<--- Score

207. Who is responsible for ensuring appropriate resources (time, people and money) are allocated to Virtual Desktop Infrastructure Monitoring?

<--- Score

208. Who sets the Virtual Desktop Infrastructure Monitoring standards?

<--- Score

209. What may be the consequences for the performance of an organization if all stakeholders are not consulted regarding Virtual Desktop Infrastructure Monitoring?

<--- Score

210. How do we Lead with Virtual Desktop Infrastructure Monitoring in Mind?

<--- Score

211. What is an unauthorized commitment?

<--- Score

212. What are the success criteria that will indicate that Virtual Desktop Infrastructure Monitoring objectives have been met and the benefits delivered?

<--- Score

213. How can we become more high-tech but still be high touch?

<--- Score

214. What role does communication play in the success or failure of a Virtual Desktop Infrastructure Monitoring project?

<--- Score

215. What is our question?

<--- Score

216. What are the Essentials of Internal Virtual Desktop Infrastructure Monitoring Management?

<--- Score

217. Whose voice (department, ethnic group, women, older workers, etc) might you have missed hearing

from in your company, and how might you amplify
this voice to create positive momentum for your
business?
<--- Score

Add up total points for this section:
_____ = Total points for this section

Divided by: _____ (number of
statements answered) = _____
Average score for this section

Transfer your score to the Virtual
Desktop Infrastructure Monitoring
Index at the beginning of the Self-
Assessment.

Virtual Desktop Infrastructure Monitoring and Managing Projects, Criteria for Project Managers:

1.0 Initiating Process Group: Virtual Desktop Infrastructure Monitoring

1. Were decisions made in a timely manner?

2. The process to Manage Stakeholders is part of which process group?

3. What are the pressing issues of the hour?

4. What are the short and long term implications?

5. What do they need to know about the Virtual Desktop Infrastructure Monitoring project?

6. What communication items need improvement?

7. What were things that you did well, but could improve, and how?

8. At which CMMI level are software processes documented, standardized, and integrated into a standard to-be practiced process for your organization?

9. Measurable - Are the targets measurable?

10. Do you understand the quality and control criteria that must be achieved for successful Virtual Desktop Infrastructure Monitoring project completion?

11. What will you do to minimize the impact should a risk event occur?

12. What are the required resources?

13. What areas were overlooked on this Virtual Desktop Infrastructure Monitoring project?

14. Are stakeholders properly informed about the status of the Virtual Desktop Infrastructure Monitoring project?

15. Am I just doing busywork to pass the time?

16. Do you know all the stakeholders impacted by the Virtual Desktop Infrastructure Monitoring project and what their needs are?

17. Did you use a contractor or vendor?

18. Are you properly tracking the progress of the Virtual Desktop Infrastructure Monitoring project and communicating the status to stakeholders?

19. Specific - Is the objective clear in terms of what, how, when, and where the situation will be changed?

20. Which of Six Sigmas DMAIC phases focuses on the measurement of internal process that affect factors that are critical to quality?

1.1 Project Charter: Virtual Desktop Infrastructure Monitoring

21. Why is a Virtual Desktop Infrastructure Monitoring project Charter used?

22. Why have you chosen the aim you have set forth?

23. How are Virtual Desktop Infrastructure Monitoring projects different from Operations?

24. Success Determination Factors: How will the success of the Virtual Desktop Infrastructure Monitoring project be determined from the customers perspective?

25. How will you know that a change is an improvement?

26. What are you striving to accomplish (measurable goal(s))?

27. What are the assumptions?

28. Run it as as a startup?

29. What are the known stakeholder requirements?

30. Who is the Virtual Desktop Infrastructure Monitoring project Manager?

31. What is the justification?

32. How high should you set our goals?

33. What's in it for you?

34. Is it an improvement over existing products?

35. What are the constraints?

36. Who will take notes, document decisions?

37. Who are the stakeholders?

38. Assumptions: What factors, for planning purposes, are you considering to be true?

39. Must Have?

40. Who Manages Integration?

1.2 Stakeholder Register: Virtual Desktop Infrastructure Monitoring

41. How will Reports Be Created?

42. Who is Managing Stakeholder Engagement?

43. Is Your Organization Ready for Change?

44. How should employers make their voices heard?

45. What is the power of the stakeholder?

46. What opportunities exist to provide communications?

47. How Big is the Gap?

48. What & Why?

49. What are the major Virtual Desktop Infrastructure Monitoring project milestones requiring communications or providing communications opportunities?

50. Who wants to talk about Security?

51. How much influence do they have on the Virtual Desktop Infrastructure Monitoring project?

1.3 Stakeholder Analysis Matrix: Virtual Desktop Infrastructure Monitoring

52. What is the organizations competitors doing?

53. Partnership opportunities/synergies?

54. Advantages of proposition?

55. Contributions to policy and practice?

56. Which resources are required?

57. What is the stakeholders power and status in relation to the Virtual Desktop Infrastructure Monitoring project?

58. What is our Advocacy Strategy?

59. Is there a clear description of the scope of practice of the Virtual Desktop Infrastructure Monitoring projects educators?

60. What actions can be taken to reduce or mitigate risk?

61. Are they likely to influence the success or failure of your Virtual Desktop Infrastructure Monitoring project?

62. Resources, Assets, People?

63. Vital contracts and partners?

64. What do the orgabizations stakeholders do better than anyone else?

65. How do you manage Virtual Desktop Infrastructure Monitoring project Risk?

66. How are you predicting what future (work)loads will be?

67. Who is directly responsible for decisions on issues important to the Virtual Desktop Infrastructure Monitoring project?

68. Who has not been involved up to now but should have been?

69. Is changing technology threatening our organizations position?

70. Location and geographical?

2.0 Planning Process Group: Virtual Desktop Infrastructure Monitoring

71. Will you be replaced?

72. In what way has the Virtual Desktop Infrastructure Monitoring project come up with innovative measures for problem-solving?

73. Mitigate. What will you do to minimize the impact should a risk event occur?

74. Did you read it correctly?

75. What Will You Do?

76. Is the pace of implementing the products of the programme ensuring the completeness of the results of the Virtual Desktop Infrastructure Monitoring project?

77. What is the NEXT thing to do?

78. To what extent have public/private national resources and/or counterparts been mobilized to contribute to the programmes objective and produce results and impacts?

79. Virtual Desktop Infrastructure Monitoring project Assessment; Why did you do this Virtual Desktop Infrastructure Monitoring project?

80. How well will the chosen processes produce the

expected results?

81. If a task is partitionable, is this a sufficient condition to reduce the Virtual Desktop Infrastructure Monitoring project duration?

82. To what extent have the target population and participants made the activities their own, taking an active role in it?

83. In which Virtual Desktop Infrastructure Monitoring project management process group is the detailed Virtual Desktop Infrastructure Monitoring project budget created?

84. How well defined and documented are the Virtual Desktop Infrastructure Monitoring project management processes you chose to use?

85. Just how important is your work to the overall success of the Virtual Desktop Infrastructure Monitoring project?

86. How many days can task X be late in starting without affecting the Virtual Desktop Infrastructure Monitoring project completion date?

87. How does activity resource estimation affect activity duration estimation?

88. What is the critical path for this Virtual Desktop Infrastructure Monitoring project, and what is the duration of the critical path?

89. In what way has the program contributed towards the issue culture and development included on the

public agenda?

2.1 Project Management Plan: Virtual Desktop Infrastructure Monitoring

90. Why Change?

91. Does the implementation plan have an appropriate division of responsibilities?

92. Are comparable cost estimates used for comparing, screening and selecting alternative plans, and has a reasonable cost estimate been developed for the recommended plan?

93. Did the planning effort collaborate to develop solutions that integrate expertise, policies, programs, and Virtual Desktop Infrastructure Monitoring projects across entities?

94. Who is the sponsor?

95. Why Do you Manage Integration?

96. When is the Virtual Desktop Infrastructure Monitoring project management plan created?

97. What would you do differently?

98. Where does all this information come from?

99. Was the peer (technical) review of the cost estimates duly coordinated with the cost estimate center of expertise and addressed in the review documentation and certification?

100. Are there any windfall benefits that would accrue to the Virtual Desktop Infrastructure Monitoring project sponsor or other parties?

101. What happened during the process that you found interesting?

102. Are calculations and results of analyses essentially correct?

103. What is the business need?

104. What if, for example, the positive direction and vision of the organization causes expected trends to change resulting in greater need than expected?

105. Is there an incremental analysis/cost effectiveness analysis of proposed mitigation features based on an approved method and using an accepted model?

106. What should you drop in order to add something new?

107. Are there any client staffing expectations?

2.2 Scope Management Plan: Virtual Desktop Infrastructure Monitoring

108. How difficult will it be to do specific activities on this Virtual Desktop Infrastructure Monitoring project?

109. Have the personnel with the necessary skills and competence been identified and has agreement for their participation in the Virtual Desktop Infrastructure Monitoring project been reached with the appropriate management?

110. Quality Standards - Are controls in place to ensure that the work was not only completed but also completed to meet specific standards?

111. What are the risks that could significantly affect the schedule of the Virtual Desktop Infrastructure Monitoring project?

112. Are the appropriate IT resources adequate to meet planned commitments?

113. Pop Quiz – Which are the same inputs as in Scope Planning?

114. Will anyone else be involved in verifying the deliverables?

115. Is the schedule updated on a periodic basis?

116. Is there any form of automated support for Issues Management?

117. Time estimation – how much time will be needed?

118. Are there any scope changes proposed for the previously authorized Virtual Desktop Infrastructure Monitoring project?

119. Product – what are you trying to accomplish and how will you know when you are finished?

120. Process Groups – where do Scope Management Processes fit in?

121. Have all documents been archived in a Virtual Desktop Infrastructure Monitoring project repository for each release?

122. What are the risks that could significantly affect the resources needed for the Virtual Desktop Infrastructure Monitoring project?

123. To whom will the deliverables be first presented for inspection and verification?

124. Have activity relationships and interdependencies within tasks been adequately identified?

125. Is there a Virtual Desktop Infrastructure Monitoring project organization chart showing the reporting relationships and responsibilities for each position?

126. Has a Quality Assurance Plan been developed for the Virtual Desktop Infrastructure Monitoring project?

127. What happens if scope changes?

2.3 Requirements Management Plan: Virtual Desktop Infrastructure Monitoring

128. Who will do the reporting and to whom will reports be delivered?

129. Do you know which stakeholders will participate in the requirements effort?

130. Is infrastructure setup part of your Virtual Desktop Infrastructure Monitoring project?

131. Will the contractors involved take full responsibility?

132. Who is responsible for quantifying the Virtual Desktop Infrastructure Monitoring project requirements?

133. Do you have price sheets and a methodology for determining the total proposal cost?

134. Did you use declarative statements?

135. Is Requirements work dependent on any other specific Virtual Desktop Infrastructure Monitoring project or non-Virtual Desktop Infrastructure Monitoring project activities (e.g. funding, approvals, procurement)?

136. To see if a requirement statement is sufficiently well-defined, read it from the developer's perspective.

Mentally add the phrase, "call me when you're done" to the end of the requirement and see if that makes you nervous. In other words, would you need additional clarification from the author to understand the requirement well enough to design and implement it?

137. Is the Change Control process documented?

138. How will the requirements become prioritized?

139. Controlling Virtual Desktop Infrastructure Monitoring project requirements involves monitoring the status of the Virtual Desktop Infrastructure Monitoring project requirements and managing changes to the requirements. Who is responsible for monitoring and tracking the Virtual Desktop Infrastructure Monitoring project requirements?

140. Have stakeholders been instructed in the Change Control process?

141. Will the product release be stable and mature enough to be deployed in the user community?

142. After the requirements are gathered and set forth on the requirements register, they're little more than a laundry list of items. Some may be duplicates, some might conflict with others and some will be too broad or too vague to understand. Describe how the requirements will be analyzed. Who will perform the analysis?

143. What are you counting on?

144. Who will finally present the work or product(s) for

acceptance?

145. Who will initially review the Virtual Desktop Infrastructure Monitoring project work or products to ensure it meets the applicable acceptance criteria?

146. Did you distinguish the scope of work the contractor(s) will be required to do?

147. Should you include sub-activities?

2.4 Requirements Documentation: Virtual Desktop Infrastructure Monitoring

148. How much testing do you need to do to prove that my system is safe?

149. How will they be documented / shared?

150. How can you document system requirements?

151. Completeness. Are all functions required by the customer included?

152. Consistency. Are there any requirements conflicts?

153. Have the benefits identified with the system being identified clearly?

154. Is your Business Case still valid?

155. Basic work/Business process; high-level, what is being touched?

156. Are there legal issues?

157. Are there any requirements conflicts?

158. Who provides requirements?

159. How will Requirements be documented and who signs off on them?

160. Verifiability. Can the requirements be checked?

161. What is your Elevator Speech?

162. What is Effective documentation?

163. What marketing channels do you want to use: e-mail, letter or sms?

164. The problem with gathering requirements is right there in the word gathering. What images does it conjure?

165. How will the proposed Virtual Desktop Infrastructure Monitoring project help?

166. Does your company restrict technical alternatives?

167. Can you Check System Requirements?

2.5 Requirements Traceability Matrix: Virtual Desktop Infrastructure Monitoring

168. What is the WBS?

169. Describe the process for approving requirements so they can be added to the traceability matrix and Virtual Desktop Infrastructure Monitoring project work can be performed. Will the Virtual Desktop Infrastructure Monitoring project requirements become approved in writing?

170. Why use a WBS?

171. What are the chronologies, contingencies, consequences, criteria?

172. How will it affect the stakeholders personally in their career?

173. What percentage of Virtual Desktop Infrastructure Monitoring projects are producing traceability matrices between requirements and other work products?

174. Is there a requirements traceability process in place?

175. Do we have a clear understanding of all subcontracts in place?

176. Why Do you Manage Scope?

177. Will you use a Requirements Traceability Matrix?

178. How small is small enough?

179. How Do you Manage Scope?

2.6 Project Scope Statement: Virtual Desktop Infrastructure Monitoring

180. Are there backup strategies for key members of the Virtual Desktop Infrastructure Monitoring project?

181. What actions will be taken to mitigate the risk?

182. What Went Wrong?

183. Is there an information system for the Virtual Desktop Infrastructure Monitoring project?

184. Were key Virtual Desktop Infrastructure Monitoring project stakeholders brought into the Virtual Desktop Infrastructure Monitoring project Plan?

185. Name and describe the 2 elements of scope management that deal with concept development ?

186. Where and How Does the Team Fit Within the Organization Structure?

187. Is the plan for Virtual Desktop Infrastructure Monitoring project resources adequate?

188. Is there a process (test plans, inspections, reviews) defined for verifying outputs for each task?

189. Have the Configuration Management functions been assigned?

190. Are there completion/verification criteria defined for each task producing an output?

191. Will the Risk Status be reported to management on a regular and frequent basis?

192. Identify how your team and you will create the Virtual Desktop Infrastructure Monitoring project scope statement and the work breakdown structure (WBS). Document how you will create the Virtual Desktop Infrastructure Monitoring project scope statement and WBS, and make sure you answer the following questions: In defining Virtual Desktop Infrastructure Monitoring project scope and the WBS, will you and your Virtual Desktop Infrastructure Monitoring project team be using methods defined by your organization, methods defined by the Virtual Desktop Infrastructure Monitoring project management office (PMO), or other methods?

193. Name and describe the 2 elements that deal with providing the detail?

194. Are there specific processes you will use to evaluate and approve/reject changes?

195. Are the meetings set up to have assigned note takers that will add action/issues to the issue list?

196. Will there be a Change Control Process in place?

197. What is the most common tool for helping define the detail?

198. Was planning completed before the Virtual Desktop Infrastructure Monitoring project was

initiated?

2.7 Assumption and Constraint Log: Virtual Desktop Infrastructure Monitoring

199. How are new requirements or changes to requirements identified?

200. Are processes for release management of new development from coding and unit testing, to integration testing, to training, and production defined and followed?

201. Are there processes in place to ensure internal consistency between the source code components?

202. What do you audit?

203. What other teams / processes would be impacted by changes to the current process, and how?

204. What Threats might prevent us from getting there?

205. Does the traceability documentation describe the tool and/or mechanism to be used to capture traceability throughout the life cycle?

206. Does the Virtual Desktop Infrastructure Monitoring project have a formal Virtual Desktop Infrastructure Monitoring project Plan?

207. Contradictory information between document sections?

208. How can constraints be violated?

209. Was the document/deliverable developed per the appropriate or required standards (for example, Institute of Electrical and Electronics Engineers standards)?

210. Have Virtual Desktop Infrastructure Monitoring project management standards and procedures been established and documented?

211. What Strengths do you have?

212. When can log be discarded?

213. Is the amount of effort justified by the anticipated value of forming a new process?

214. Are formal code reviews conducted?

215. Have you eliminated all duplicative tasks or manual efforts, where appropriate?

216. Are there ways to reduce the time it takes to get something approved?

217. Does a documented Virtual Desktop Infrastructure Monitoring project organizational policy & plan (i.e. governance model) exist?

218. After observing execution of process, is it in compliance with the documented Plan?

2.8 Work Breakdown Structure: Virtual Desktop Infrastructure Monitoring

219. When would you develop a Work Breakdown Structure?

220. Who has to do it?

221. What has to be done?

222. How big is a work-package?

223. Is it still viable?

224. Can you make it?

225. How much detail?

226. Do you need another level?

227. What is the probability of completing the Virtual Desktop Infrastructure Monitoring project in less that xx days?

228. What is the probability that the Virtual Desktop Infrastructure Monitoring project duration will exceed xx weeks?

229. Is it a change in scope?

230. When do you stop?

231. When does it have to be done?

232. Is the Work breakdown Structure (WBS) defined and is the scope of the Virtual Desktop Infrastructure Monitoring project clear with assigned deliverable owners?

233. How Far Down?

234. Where does it take place?

235. How many levels?

236. Why would you develop a Work Breakdown Structure?

237. Why is it useful?

238. How will you and your Virtual Desktop Infrastructure Monitoring project team define the Virtual Desktop Infrastructure Monitoring projects scope and work breakdown structure?

2.9 WBS Dictionary: Virtual Desktop Infrastructure Monitoring

239. What is the end result of a work package?

240. Contemplated overhead expenditure for each period based on the best information currently available?

241. Wbs elements contractually specified for reporting of status to us (lowest level only)?

242. Are data elements summarized through the functional organizational structure for progressively higher levels of management?

243. Do the lines of authority for incurring indirect costs correspond to the lines of responsibility for management control of the same components of costs?

244. Identify potential or actual overruns and underruns?

245. Changes in the overhead pool and/or organization structures?

246. Are overhead cost budgets established for each organization which has authority to incur overhead costs?

247. Detailed schedules which support control account and work package start and completion

dates/events?

248. Can the contractor substantiate work package and planning package budgets?

249. Are detailed work packages planned as far in advance as practicable?

250. Does the contractor require sufficient detailed planning of control accounts to constrain the application of budget initially allocated for future effort to current effort?

251. Identify and isolate causes of favorable and unfavorable cost and schedule variances?

252. Where engineering standards or other internal work measurement systems are used, is there a formal relationship between these values and work package budgets?

253. Are the contractors estimates of costs at completion reconcilable with cost data reported to us?

254. Time-phased control account budgets?

255. Are the WBS and organizational levels for application of the Virtual Desktop Infrastructure Monitoring projected overhead costs identified?

256. Are all authorized tasks assigned to identified organizational elements?

257. What size should a work package be?

2.10 Schedule Management Plan: Virtual Desktop Infrastructure Monitoring

258. Have the procedures for identifying budget variances been followed?

259. Are assumptions being identified, recorded, analyzed, qualified and closed?

260. Are tasks tracked by hours?

261. Are adequate resources provided for the quality assurance function?

262. Has a provision been made to reassess Virtual Desktop Infrastructure Monitoring project risks at various Virtual Desktop Infrastructure Monitoring project stages?

263. Are mitigation strategies identified?

264. Do Virtual Desktop Infrastructure Monitoring project managers participating in the Virtual Desktop Infrastructure Monitoring project know the Virtual Desktop Infrastructure Monitoring projects true status first hand?

265. Has a Resource Management Plan been created?

266. Are all resource assumptions documented?

267. Timeline and milestones?

268. Is PERT / Critical Path or equivalent methodology being used?

269. Has the budget been baselined?

270. Has a Quality Assurance Plan been developed for the Virtual Desktop Infrastructure Monitoring project?

271. Is the correct WBS element identified for each task and milestone in the IMS?

272. Is there an on-going process in place to monitor Virtual Desktop Infrastructure Monitoring project risks?

273. Cost / Benefit Analysis?

274. Have Virtual Desktop Infrastructure Monitoring project success criteria been defined?

275. Was the scope definition used in task sequencing?

276. Have all unresolved risks been documented?

277. Were Virtual Desktop Infrastructure Monitoring project team members involved in detailed estimating and scheduling?

2.11 Activity List: Virtual Desktop Infrastructure Monitoring

278. How should ongoing costs be monitored to try to keep the Virtual Desktop Infrastructure Monitoring project within budget?

279. Where will it be performed?

280. Is infrastructure setup part of your Virtual Desktop Infrastructure Monitoring project?

281. What Went Right?

282. Is there anything planned that doesn t need to be here?

283. The WBS is developed as part of a Joint Planning session. But how do you know that youve done this right?

284. What will be performed?

285. For other activities, how much delay can be tolerated?

286. How detailed should a Virtual Desktop Infrastructure Monitoring project get?

287. How can the Virtual Desktop Infrastructure Monitoring project be displayed graphically to better visualize the activities?

288. Who will perform the work?

289. In what sequence?

290. Are the required resources available or need to be acquired?

291. How difficult will it be to do specific activities on this Virtual Desktop Infrastructure Monitoring project?

292. How much slack is available in the Virtual Desktop Infrastructure Monitoring project?

293. What is the probability the Virtual Desktop Infrastructure Monitoring project can be completed in xx weeks?

294. What is the total time required to complete the Virtual Desktop Infrastructure Monitoring project if no delays occur?

295. When will the work be performed?

296. Can you determine the activity that must finish, before this activity can start?

2.12 Activity Attributes: Virtual Desktop Infrastructure Monitoring

297. Are the required resources available?

298. Activity: Whats In the Bag?

299. Were there other ways you could have organized the data to achieve similar results?

300. Why?

301. Have you identified the Activity Leveling Priority code value on each activity?

302. How many resources do you need to complete the work scope within a limit of X number of days?

303. What activity do you think you should spend the most time on?

304. What conclusions/generalizations can you draw from this?

305. How difficult will it be to complete specific activities on this Virtual Desktop Infrastructure Monitoring project?

306. Activity: Fair or Not Fair?

307. How many days do you need to complete the work scope with a limit of X number of resources?

308. Which method produces the more accurate cost assignment?

309. How difficult will it be to do specific activities on this Virtual Desktop Infrastructure Monitoring project?

310. Resources to accomplish the work?

311. Time for overtime?

312. Have constraints been applied to the start and finish milestones for the phases?

313. Would you consider either of these activities an outlier?

2.13 Milestone List: Virtual Desktop Infrastructure Monitoring

314. Continuity, supply chain robustness?

315. Obstacles faced?

316. Describe the industry you are in and the market growth opportunities. What is the market for your technology, product or service?

317. Political effects?

318. Reliability of data, plan predictability?

319. How late can the activity finish?

320. Timescales, deadlines and pressures?

321. How will you get the word out to customers?

322. Global influences?

323. Can you derive how soon can the whole Virtual Desktop Infrastructure Monitoring project finish?

324. Calculate how long can activity be delayed?

325. Information and research?

326. How soon can the activity start?

327. Milestone pages should display the UserID of the

person who added the milestone. Does a report or query exist that provides this audit information?

328. New USPs?

329. Effects on core activities, distraction?

330. How difficult will it be to do specific activities on this Virtual Desktop Infrastructure Monitoring project?

331. How Do you Manage Time?

332. How soon can the activity finish?

333. What is the organization s history in doing similar activities?

2.14 Network Diagram: Virtual Desktop Infrastructure Monitoring

334. What is the completion time?

335. What are the tools?

336. What are the Major Administrative Issues?

337. Where do you schedule uncertainty time?

338. What job or jobs could run concurrently?

339. Can you calculate the confidence level?

340. What activities must occur simultaneously with this activity?

341. Will crashing x weeks return more in benefits than it costs?

342. What activity must be completed immediately before this activity can start?

343. How confident can you be in our milestone dates and the delivery date?

344. What controls the start and finish of a job?

345. Are the Gantt Chart and/or Network Diagram updated periodically and used to assess the overall Virtual Desktop Infrastructure Monitoring project timetable?

346. Which type of network diagram allows you to depict four types of dependencies?

347. What is the probability of completing the Virtual Desktop Infrastructure Monitoring project in less that xx days?

348. What job or jobs follow it?

349. What is the lowest cost to complete this Virtual Desktop Infrastructure Monitoring project in xx weeks?

350. How difficult will it be to do specific activities on this Virtual Desktop Infrastructure Monitoring project?

351. What to do and When?

2.15 Activity Resource Requirements: Virtual Desktop Infrastructure Monitoring

352. When does Monitoring Begin?

353. Which logical relationship does the PDM use most often?

354. Are there unresolved issues that need to be addressed?

355. What is the Work Plan Standard?

356. Do you use tools like decomposition and rolling-wave planning to produce the activity list and other outputs?

357. Why do you do that?

358. Other support in specific areas?

359. Anything else?

360. How do you handle petty cash?

361. How many signatures do you require on a check and does this match what is in your policy and procedures?

362. What are constraints that you might find during the Human Resource Planning process?

363. Organizational Applicability?

2.16 Resource Breakdown Structure: Virtual Desktop Infrastructure Monitoring

364. Why is this important?

365. What is the number one predictor of a groups productivity?

366. What is the organizations history in doing similar activities?

367. What is the purpose of assigning and documenting responsibility?

368. Who needs what information?

369. What is the primary purpose of the human resource plan?

370. Is Predictive Resource Analysis being done?

371. What is each stakeholders desired outcome for the Virtual Desktop Infrastructure Monitoring project?

372. Who will be used as a Virtual Desktop Infrastructure Monitoring project team member?

373. Any Changes from Stakeholders?

374. What s the difference between % Complete and % work?

375. How difficult will it be to do specific activities on this Virtual Desktop Infrastructure Monitoring project?

376. Which resource planning tool provides information on resource responsibility and accountability?

377. What Defines a Successful Virtual Desktop Infrastructure Monitoring project?

378. Which resources should be in the resource pool?

379. What are the requirements for resource data?

380. Who is allowed to perform which functions?

381. How should the information be delivered?

2.17 Activity Duration Estimates: Virtual Desktop Infrastructure Monitoring

382. What are the three main outputs of quality control?

383. Is the work performed reviewed against contractual objectives?

384. Which is TRUE if activity B actually takes 37 hours?

385. What is the difference between using brainstorming and the Delphi technique for risk identification?

386. What are the main parts of a scope statement?

387. Which is the BEST thing to do to try to complete a Virtual Desktop Infrastructure Monitoring project two days earlier?

388. What should be done NEXT?

389. Are procurement documents used to solicit accurate and complete proposals from prospective sellers?

390. Which would be the NEXT thing for the Virtual Desktop Infrastructure Monitoring project manager to do?

391. Why is outsourcing growing so rapidly?

392. Is earned value analysis completed to assess Virtual Desktop Infrastructure Monitoring project performance?

393. Which skills do you think are most important for an information technology Virtual Desktop Infrastructure Monitoring project manager?

394. Are Virtual Desktop Infrastructure Monitoring project results verified and Virtual Desktop Infrastructure Monitoring project documents archived?

395. Research recruiting and retention strategies at three different companies. What distinguishes one company from another in this area?

396. Why do you think schedule issues often cause the most conflicts on Virtual Desktop Infrastructure Monitoring projects?

397. Where Do Schedules Come From?

398. What are some of the options you found to help people prepare for the exam?

399. Do you think many information technology professionals have experience writing RFPs and evaluating proposals for information technology Virtual Desktop Infrastructure Monitoring projects?

400. Do stakeholders follow a procedure for formally accepting the Virtual Desktop Infrastructure Monitoring project scope?

401. Does a process exist to identify which qualified resources may be attainable?

2.18 Duration Estimating Worksheet: Virtual Desktop Infrastructure Monitoring

402. What is the probability the Virtual Desktop Infrastructure Monitoring project can be completed in 47 weeks?

403. Why estimate time and cost?

404. What s Next?

405. What is the total time required to complete the Virtual Desktop Infrastructure Monitoring project if no delays occur?

406. How should ongoing costs be monitored to try to keep the Virtual Desktop Infrastructure Monitoring project within budget?

407. Is a Construction detail attached (to aid in explanation)?

408. Is this operation cost effective?

409. What does it mean to say a task is 75% complete after 3 months?

410. Done before proceeding with this activity or what can be done concurrently?

411. Does the Virtual Desktop Infrastructure Monitoring project provide innovative ways for

Veterans to overcome obstacles or deliver better outcomes?

412. What work will be included in the Virtual Desktop Infrastructure Monitoring project?

413. What utility impacts are there?

414. What is the least expensive way to complete the Virtual Desktop Infrastructure Monitoring project within 40 weeks?

415. Value Pocket Identification & Quantification What Are Value Pockets?

416. What are the critical bottleneck activities?

417. Do any colleagues have experience with the company and/or RFPs?

418. How can the Virtual Desktop Infrastructure Monitoring project be displayed graphically to better visualize the activities?

419. What questions do you have?

2.19 Project Schedule: Virtual Desktop Infrastructure Monitoring

420. To what degree is do you feel the entire team was committed to the Virtual Desktop Infrastructure Monitoring project schedule?

421. Meet requirements?

422. Why do you need to manage Virtual Desktop Infrastructure Monitoring project Risk?

423. Whats the difference?

424. How long does a 12 month Virtual Desktop Infrastructure Monitoring project take?

425. What does that mean?

426. How can slack be negative?

427. Is the Virtual Desktop Infrastructure Monitoring project schedule available for all Virtual Desktop Infrastructure Monitoring project team members to review?

428. Is the structure for tracking the Virtual Desktop Infrastructure Monitoring project schedule well defined and assigned to a specific individual?

429. Understand the constraints used in preparing the schedule. Are activities connected because logic dictates the order in which others occur?

430. What is Virtual Desktop Infrastructure Monitoring project Management?

431. Why do you think schedule issues often cause the most conflicts on Virtual Desktop Infrastructure Monitoring projects?

432. How does a Virtual Desktop Infrastructure Monitoring project get to be a year late ?

433. Virtual Desktop Infrastructure Monitoring project work estimates Who is managing the work estimate quality of work tasks in the Virtual Desktop Infrastructure Monitoring project schedule?

434. What documents, if any, will the subcontractor provide (eg Virtual Desktop Infrastructure Monitoring project schedule, quality plan etc)?

435. How much slack is available in the Virtual Desktop Infrastructure Monitoring project?

2.20 Cost Management Plan: Virtual Desktop Infrastructure Monitoring

436. Does the detailed Virtual Desktop Infrastructure Monitoring project plan identify individual responsibilities for the next 4–6 weeks?

437. How difficult will it be to do specific tasks on the Virtual Desktop Infrastructure Monitoring project?

438. What are the Virtual Desktop Infrastructure Monitoring project objectives?

439. Were Virtual Desktop Infrastructure Monitoring project team members involved in detailed estimating and scheduling?

440. Are quality inspections and review activities listed in the Virtual Desktop Infrastructure Monitoring project schedule(s)?

441. How does the proposed individual meet each requirement?

442. Has Virtual Desktop Infrastructure Monitoring project success criteria been defined?

443. Scope of work – What is the likelihood and extent of potential future changes to the Virtual Desktop Infrastructure Monitoring project scope?

444. Is a Stakeholder Management plan in place that covers topics?

445. Does the Business Case include how the Virtual Desktop Infrastructure Monitoring project aligns with the organizations strategic goals & objectives?

446. Contingency – How will cost contingency be administered?

447. Are schedule deliverables actually delivered?

448. Are meeting minutes captured and sent out after the meeting?

449. Was the Virtual Desktop Infrastructure Monitoring project schedule reviewed by all stakeholders and formally accepted?

450. Is the Virtual Desktop Infrastructure Monitoring project Sponsor clearly communicating the Business Case or rationale for why this Virtual Desktop Infrastructure Monitoring project is needed?

451. Is there an approved case?

452. Are the results of quality assurance reviews provided to affected groups & individuals?

453. Who will prepare the cost estimates?

2.21 Activity Cost Estimates: Virtual Desktop Infrastructure Monitoring

454. What is included in indirect cost being allocated?

455. Does the estimator have experience?

456. What is Virtual Desktop Infrastructure Monitoring project Cost Management?

457. What procedures are put in place regarding bidding and cost comparisons, if any?

458. Review – what are some common errors in activities to avoid?

459. What areas were overlooked on this Virtual Desktop Infrastructure Monitoring project?

460. Does the estimator estimate by task or by person?

461. Why Do you Manage Cost?

462. Estimated cost?

463. How Do you Manage Cost?

464. What is the activity inventory?

465. Does the activity use a common approach or business function to deliver its results?

466. What are you looking for?

467. Based on your Virtual Desktop Infrastructure Monitoring project communication management plan, what worked well?

468. Were sponsors and decision makers available when needed outside regularly scheduled meetings?

469. How Award?

470. What is a Virtual Desktop Infrastructure Monitoring project Management Plan?

471. What are the audit requirements?

472. How do you treat administrative costs in the activity inventory?

473. Did the consultant work with local staff to develop local capacity?

2.22 Cost Estimating Worksheet: Virtual Desktop Infrastructure Monitoring

474. What is the estimated labor cost today based upon this information?

475. Is the Virtual Desktop Infrastructure Monitoring project responsive to community need?

476. Is it feasible to establish a control group arrangement?

477. What costs are to be estimated?

478. What is the purpose of estimating?

479. How will the results be shared and to whom?

480. Identify the timeframe necessary to monitor progress and collect data to determine how the selected measure has changed?

481. Ask: are others positioned to know, are others credible, and will others cooperate?

482. What info is needed?

483. What will others want?

484. Will the Virtual Desktop Infrastructure Monitoring project collaborate with the local community and leverage resources?

485. Can a trend be established from historical performance data on the selected measure and are the criteria for using trend analysis or forecasting methods met?

486. What additional Virtual Desktop Infrastructure Monitoring project(s) could be initiated as a result of this Virtual Desktop Infrastructure Monitoring project?

487. Who is best positioned to know and assist in identifying such factors?

488. What Can Be Included?

489. What happens to any remaining funds not used?

490. Does the Virtual Desktop Infrastructure Monitoring project provide innovative ways for stakeholders to overcome obstacles or deliver better outcomes?

2.23 Cost Baseline: Virtual Desktop Infrastructure Monitoring

491. Is there anything unique in this Virtual Desktop Infrastructure Monitoring project s scope statement that will affect resources?

492. Has operations management formally accepted responsibility for operating and maintaining the product(s) or service(s) delivered by the Virtual Desktop Infrastructure Monitoring project?

493. Virtual Desktop Infrastructure Monitoring project Goals -should others be reconsidered?

494. Suppose you were buying 10 PCs for your new business. What would some of the life cycle costs be?

495. Does the suggested change request seem to represent a necessary enhancement to the product?

496. Who will use such metrics ?

497. Is the requested change request a result of changes in other Virtual Desktop Infrastructure Monitoring project(s)?

498. Has training and knowledge transfer of the operations organization been completed?

499. Does the suggested change request represent a desired enhancement to the products functionality?

500. How fast?

501. Have the actual milestone completion dates been compared to the approved schedule?

502. How long are you willing to wait before you find out were late?

503. On budget?

504. Has the Virtual Desktop Infrastructure Monitoring projected annual cost to operate and maintain the product(s) or service(s) been approved and funded?

505. Have all approved changes to the cost baseline been identified and impact on the Virtual Desktop Infrastructure Monitoring project documented?

506. How concrete were original objectives?

507. Has the documentation relating to operation and maintenance of the product(s) or service(s) been delivered to, and accepted by, operations management?

508. Does it impact schedule, cost, quality?

509. Are you meeting with your team regularly?

510. What would some of the life cycle costs be?

2.24 Quality Management Plan: Virtual Desktop Infrastructure Monitoring

511. How are changes to procedures made?

512. List your organizations customer contact standards that employees are expected to maintain. How are such standards measured?

513. How many Virtual Desktop Infrastructure Monitoring project staff does this specific process affect?

514. How effectively was the Quality Management Plan applied during Virtual Desktop Infrastructure Monitoring project Execution?

515. Is there a procedure for this process?

516. How does your organization decide what to measure?

517. Checking the completeness and appropriateness of the sampling and testing. Were the right locations/ samples tested for the right parameters?

518. How do you decide what information needs to be recorded?

519. Are there standards for code development?

520. What is Quality Planning ?

521. Has a Virtual Desktop Infrastructure Monitoring project Communications Plan been developed?

522. How do senior leaders review organizational performance?

523. How are calibration records kept?

524. Does the program use other agents to collect samples?

525. Does a prospective decision remain the same regardless of what the data shows?

526. What are your organizations current levels and trends for those measures related to employee wellbeing, satisfaction, and development?

527. How does your organization design processes to ensure others meet customer and others requirements?

528. How are such standards measured?

529. How does your organization ensure the quality, reliability, and user-friendliness of its hardware and software?

2.25 Quality Metrics: Virtual Desktop Infrastructure Monitoring

530. Which are the right metrics to use?

531. How does one achieve stability?

532. What is the benchmark?

533. What method of measurement do you use?

534. What if the biggest risk to your business were those people who dont complain?

535. How effective are your security tests?

536. Do the operators focus on determining; is there anything I need to worry about?

537. Has trace of defects been initiated?

538. When is the security analysis testing complete?

539. Are there already quality metrics available that detect nonlinear embeddings and trends similar to the users perception?

540. Were number of defects identified?

541. What happens if you get an abnormal result?

542. Did evaluation start on time?

543. Are interface issues coordinated?

544. How can the effectiveness of each of the activities be measured?

545. What metrics do you measure?

546. Is there a set of procedures to capture, analyze and act on quality metrics?

547. Did the team meet the Virtual Desktop Infrastructure Monitoring project success criteria documented in the Quality Metrics Matrix?

548. How should customers provide input?

2.26 Process Improvement Plan: Virtual Desktop Infrastructure Monitoring

549. Modeling current processes is great, but will you ever see a return on that investment?

550. What Is the Test-Cycle Concept?

551. Where do you want to be?

552. Have storage and access mechanisms and procedures been determined?

553. What personnel are the champions for the initiative?

554. Where do you focus?

555. If a Process Improvement Framework Is Being Used, Which Elements Will Help the Problems and Goals Listed?

556. Are you following the quality standards?

557. Are there forms and procedures to collect and record the data?

558. Does our process ensure quality?

559. What personnel are the coaches for your initiative?

560. Are you meeting the quality standards?

561. What personnel are the sponsors for that initiative?

562. What is quality and how will you ensure it?

563. Has the time line required to move measurement results from the points of collection to databases or users been established?

564. Who should prepare the process improvement action plan?

565. Have the frequency of collection and the points in the process where measurements will be made been determined?

566. Are you Making Progress on the Improvement Framework?

567. What makes people good SPI coaches?

568. Everyone agrees on what process improvement is, right?

2.27 Responsibility Assignment Matrix: Virtual Desktop Infrastructure Monitoring

569. Are others working on the right things?

570. Does the accounting system provide a basis for auditing records of direct costs chargeable to the contract?

571. Is work progressively subdivided into detailed work packages as requirements are defined?

572. Who is the Virtual Desktop Infrastructure Monitoring project Manager?

573. Are all elements of indirect expense identified to overhead cost budgets of Virtual Desktop Infrastructure Monitoring projections?

574. Those responsible for the establishment of budgets and assignment of resources for overhead performance?

575. Do others have the time to dedicate to your Virtual Desktop Infrastructure Monitoring project?

576. Does the contractors system identify work accomplishment against the schedule plan?

577. How many hours by each staff member/rate?

578. How do you assist them to be as productive as

possible?

579. Budgets assigned to major functional organizations?

580. Does the contractors system include procedures for measuring the performance of critical subcontractors?

581. The anticipated business volume?

582. Do managers and team members provide helpful suggestions during review meetings?

583. Are too many reports done in writing instead of verbally?

584. Does a missing responsibility indicate that the current Virtual Desktop Infrastructure Monitoring project is not yet fully understood?

585. What are the assigned resources?

586. Are estimates of costs at completion generated in a rational, consistent manner?

2.28 Roles and Responsibilities: Virtual Desktop Infrastructure Monitoring

587. What expectations were met?

588. Implementation of actions: Who are the responsible units?

589. Attainable / Achievable: The goal is attainable; can you actually accomplish the goal?

590. Concern: where are you limited or have no authority, where you cant influence?

591. What should you do now to ensure that you are meeting all expectations of your current position?

592. To decide whether to use a quality measurement, ask how will I know when it is achieved?

593. Are governance roles and responsibilities documented?

594. Was the expectation clearly communicated?

595. How well did the Virtual Desktop Infrastructure Monitoring project Team understand the expectations of specific roles and responsibilities?

596. What should you do now to prepare yourself for a promotion, increased responsibilities or a different job?

597. Is feedback clearly communicated and non-judgmental?

598. Do you take the time to clearly define roles and responsibilities on Virtual Desktop Infrastructure Monitoring project tasks?

599. Whats working well?

600. Are our budgets supportive of a culture of quality data?

601. What specific behaviors did you observe?

602. Accountabilities: What are the roles and responsibilities of individual team members?

603. What areas would you highlight for changes or improvements?

604. What should you highlight for improvement?

605. Be specific; avoid generalities. Thank you and great work alone are insufficient. What exactly do you appreciate and why?

2.29 Human Resource Management Plan: Virtual Desktop Infrastructure Monitoring

606. Is this Virtual Desktop Infrastructure Monitoring project carried out in partnership with other groups/ organizations?

607. Were the budget estimates reasonable?

608. Has the Virtual Desktop Infrastructure Monitoring project manager been identified?

609. Is Virtual Desktop Infrastructure Monitoring project status reviewed with the steering and executive teams at appropriate intervals?

610. Did the Virtual Desktop Infrastructure Monitoring project team have the right skills?

611. Is there a formal set of procedures supporting Stakeholder Management?

612. Are the key elements of a Virtual Desktop Infrastructure Monitoring project Charter present?

613. Has a provision been made to reassess Virtual Desktop Infrastructure Monitoring project risks at various Virtual Desktop Infrastructure Monitoring project stages?

614. How relevant is this attribute to this Virtual Desktop Infrastructure Monitoring project or audit?

615. Is there a requirements change management processes in place?

616. Were stakeholders aware and supportive of the principles and practices of modern cost estimation?

617. What skills, knowledge and experiences are required?

618. Does a documented Virtual Desktop Infrastructure Monitoring project organizational policy & plan (i.e. governance model) exist?

619. Is documentation created for communication with the suppliers and Vendors?

620. Have the key functions and capabilities been defined and assigned to each release or iteration?

621. Who is involved?

622. Is an industry recognized support tool(s) being used for Virtual Desktop Infrastructure Monitoring project scheduling & tracking?

623. Have all team members been part of identifying risks?

2.30 Communications Management Plan: Virtual Desktop Infrastructure Monitoring

624. Conflict Resolution -which method when?

625. Are the stakeholders getting the information others need, are others consulted, are concerns addressed?

626. Who is involved as you identify stakeholders?

627. Where do team members get information?

628. What are the interrelationships?

629. Are stakeholders internal or external?

630. What is Virtual Desktop Infrastructure Monitoring project Communications Management?

631. How Did the Term Stakeholder Originate?

632. In your work, how much time is spent on stakeholder identification?

633. Do you have members of your team responsible for certain stakeholders?

634. Who is the stakeholder?

635. Why Do you Manage Communications?

636. What to know?

637. Who to share with?

638. Is there an important stakeholder who is actively opposed and will not receive messages?

639. What is the political influence?

640. How were such initiatives successful?

641. Who did you turn to if you had questions?

642. Are you constantly rushing from meeting to meeting?

643. Do you prepare stakeholder engagement plans?

2.31 Risk Management Plan: Virtual Desktop Infrastructure Monitoring

644. Should the risk be taken at all?

645. Do you train all developers in the process?

646. Can the risk be avoided by choosing a different alternative?

647. Do the requirements require the creation of components that are unlike anything your organization has previously built?

648. Are some people working on multiple Virtual Desktop Infrastructure Monitoring projects?

649. Do requirements demand the use of new analysis, design, or testing methods?

650. Are certain activities taking a long time to complete?

651. How is Risk Monitoring Performed?

652. Is there additional information that would make you more confident about your analysis?

653. What are the chances the risk event will occur?

654. Are the participants able to keep up with the workload?

655. Are the best people available?

656. My Virtual Desktop Infrastructure Monitoring project leader has suddenly left the company, what do I do?

657. Does the customer understand the software process?

658. Does the Virtual Desktop Infrastructure Monitoring project have the authority and ability to avoid the risk?

659. Was an original risk assessment/risk management plan completed?

660. How can the process be made more effective or less cumbersome (process improvements)?

661. Are there risks to human health or the environment that need to be controlled or mitigated?

662. Maximize short-term return on investment?

663. Risks should be identified during which phase of Virtual Desktop Infrastructure Monitoring project management life cycle?

2.32 Risk Register: Virtual Desktop Infrastructure Monitoring

664. Assume the event happens, what is the Most Likely impact?

665. What has changed since the last period?

666. Risk Probability and Impact: How will the probabilities and impacts of risk items be assessed?

667. Having taken action, how did the responses effect change, and where is the Virtual Desktop Infrastructure Monitoring project now?

668. Methodology: How will risk management be performed on this Virtual Desktop Infrastructure Monitoring project?

669. Preventative actions - planned actions to reduce the likelihood a risk will occur and/or reduce the seriousness should it occur. What should you do now?

670. Who is going to do it?

671. What is the probability and impact of the risk occurring?

672. What is our current and future risk profile?

673. Can the likelihood and impact of failing to achieve such recommendations and action plans be assessed?

674. Are there other alternative controls that could be implemented?

675. What risks might negatively or positively affect achieving the Virtual Desktop Infrastructure Monitoring project objectives?

676. Contingency actions - planned actions to reduce the immediate seriousness of the risk when it does occur. What should you do when?

677. Is further information required before making a decision?

678. Who is accountable?

679. Do you require further engagement?

680. What should you do now?

681. Are corrective measures implemented as planned?

682. Recovery actions - planned actions taken once a risk has occurred to allow you to move on. What should you do after?

2.33 Probability and Impact Assessment: Virtual Desktop Infrastructure Monitoring

683. What are the risks involved in appointing external agencies to manage the Virtual Desktop Infrastructure Monitoring project?

684. Has something like this been done before?

685. How would you suggest monitoring for risk transition indicators?

686. What is the impact if the risk does occur?

687. What kind of preparation would be required to do this?

688. What are the chances the event will occur?

689. Have top software and customer managers formally committed to support the Virtual Desktop Infrastructure Monitoring project?

690. What is the probability of the risk occurring?

691. What risks does the organization have if the Virtual Desktop Infrastructure Monitoring projects fail to meet deadline?

692. Why has this particular mode of contracting been chosen?

693. What is the likely future demand of the customer?

694. Do you have a consistent repeatable process that is actually used?

695. Does the Virtual Desktop Infrastructure Monitoring project team have experience with the technology to be implemented?

696. Are Virtual Desktop Infrastructure Monitoring project requirements stable?

697. Are the software tools integrated with each other?

698. Risk Urgency Assessment -Which of your risks could occur soon, or require a longer planning time?

699. What are the industrial relations prevailing in your organization?

700. Do benefits and chances of success outweigh potential damage if success is not attained?

701. Do you manage the process through use of metrics?

2.34 Probability and Impact Matrix: Virtual Desktop Infrastructure Monitoring

702. Are team members trained in the use of the tools?

703. Are testing tools available and suitable?

704. Is the customer willing to establish rapid communication links with the developer?

705. What are the uncertainties associated with the technology selected for the Virtual Desktop Infrastructure Monitoring project?

706. What has the Virtual Desktop Infrastructure Monitoring project manager forgotten to do?

707. What will the damage be?

708. Are compilers and code generators available and suitable for the product to be built?

709. What will be the likely political environment during the life of the Virtual Desktop Infrastructure Monitoring project?

710. How do you analyse the risks in the different types of Virtual Desktop Infrastructure Monitoring projects?

711. What is the level of commitment and

professionalism?

712. Have you worked with the customer in the past?

713. How well is the risk understood?

714. What would be the effect of slippage?

715. Is there any sign of biased ranking?

716. Are the risk data complete?

717. What is Virtual Desktop Infrastructure Monitoring project Risk Management?

2.35 Risk Data Sheet: Virtual Desktop Infrastructure Monitoring

718. What was Measured?

719. Would you prefer an unknown or 70/30 chance?

720. Will revised controls lead to tolerable risk levels?

721. Do effective diagnostic tests exist?

722. What is the likelihood of it happening?

723. What are you weak at and therefore need to do better?

724. What are the main threats to our existence?

725. What are the main opportunities available to us that you should grab while you can?

726. What do people affected think about the need for, and practicality of preventive measures?

727. Has the most cost-effective solution been chosen?

728. Type of Risk Identified?

729. What were the Causes that contributed?

730. How reliable is the data source?

731. What can happen?

732. Are new hazards created?

733. Potential for Recurrence?

734. Has a sensitivity analysis been carried out?

735. What is the chance that it will happen?

736. How do you handle product safely?

737. What Do you Know?

2.36 Procurement Management Plan: Virtual Desktop Infrastructure Monitoring

738. Is there a set of procedures defining the scope, procedures, and deliverables defining quality control?

739. Were escalated issues resolved promptly?

740. Are changes in deliverable commitments agreed to by all affected groups & individuals?

741. Do you have the reasons why the changes to the organizational systems and capabilities are required?

742. Have stakeholder accountabilities & responsibilities been clearly defined?

743. Was your organizations estimating methodology being used and followed?

744. What is a Virtual Desktop Infrastructure Monitoring project Management Plan?

745. Are trade-offs between accepting the risk and mitigating the risk identified?

746. How will multiple providers be managed?

747. Are risk oriented checklists used during risk identification?

748. Do Virtual Desktop Infrastructure Monitoring

project managers participating in the Virtual Desktop Infrastructure Monitoring project know the Virtual Desktop Infrastructure Monitoring projects true status first hand?

749. Has the schedule been baselined?

750. Are target dates established for each milestone deliverable?

751. Are the Virtual Desktop Infrastructure Monitoring project plans updated on a frequent basis?

752. Are written status reports provided on a designated frequent basis?

753. Is the Virtual Desktop Infrastructure Monitoring project Sponsor clearly communicating the Business Case or rationale for why this Virtual Desktop Infrastructure Monitoring project is needed?

754. Are Virtual Desktop Infrastructure Monitoring project team members committed fulltime?

755. Are any non-compliance issues that exist communicated to the organization?

2.37 Source Selection Criteria: Virtual Desktop Infrastructure Monitoring

756. How will you evaluate offeror s proposals?

757. What Source Selection software is your team using?

758. What are Open Book debriefings?

759. Does your documentation identify why the team concurs or differs with reported performance from past performance report (CPARs, questionnaire responses, etc.)?

760. Comparison of each offer's prices to the estimated prices -are there significant differences?

761. What aspects should the contracting officer brief the Virtual Desktop Infrastructure Monitoring project on prior to evaluation of proposals?

762. What risks were identified in the proposals?

763. Is experience evaluated?

764. What are the guidelines regarding award without discussions?

765. How much weight should be placed on past performance information?

766. What is the role of counsel in the procurement

process?

767. What past performance information should be requested?

768. Does the evaluation of any change include an impact analysis; how will the change affect the scope, time, cost, and quality of the goods or services being provided?

769. If the costs are normalized, please explain how the normalization is conducted. Is a cost realism analysis used?

770. Are discussions anticipated?

771. How should oral presentations be evaluated?

772. What is price analysis and when should it be performed?

773. Do you ensure you evaluate what you asked for, not what you want to see or expect to see?

774. What management structure does the organization consider as optimal for performing the contract?

775. What Should Be Discussed?

2.38 Stakeholder Management Plan: Virtual Desktop Infrastructure Monitoring

776. Why would you develop a Virtual Desktop Infrastructure Monitoring project Business Plan?

777. Are communication systems currently in place appropriate?

778. Is it possible to track all classes of Virtual Desktop Infrastructure Monitoring project work (e.g. scheduled, un-scheduled, defect repair, etc.)?

779. Do Virtual Desktop Infrastructure Monitoring project teams & team members report on status / activities / progress?

780. How much information should be collected?

781. In your opinion, do certain Virtual Desktop Infrastructure Monitoring project resources hold a higher importance than other resources?

782. Does the Virtual Desktop Infrastructure Monitoring project have a formal Virtual Desktop Infrastructure Monitoring project Plan?

783. Are there cosmetic errors that hinder readability and comprehension?

784. What is meant by managing the triple constraint?

785. Are all Vendor contracts closed out?

786. Has a Quality Assurance Plan been developed for the Virtual Desktop Infrastructure Monitoring project?

787. Have the key elements of a coherent Virtual Desktop Infrastructure Monitoring project management strategy been established?

788. What proven methodologies and standards will be used to ensure that materials, products, processes and services are fit for their purpose?

789. Which risks pose the highest threat?

790. How, to whom and how frequently will Risk status be reported?

791. Have Virtual Desktop Infrastructure Monitoring project team accountabilities & responsibilities been clearly defined?

792. Does the detailed work plan match the complexity of tasks with the capabilities of personnel?

2.39 Change Management Plan: Virtual Desktop Infrastructure Monitoring

793. Who might present the most resistance?

794. Is it the same for each of the business units?

795. Clearly articulate the overall business benefits of the Virtual Desktop Infrastructure Monitoring project -why are you doing this now?

796. What is going to be done differently?

797. Who might be able to help us the most?

798. What does a resilient organization look like?

799. What do you expect the target audience to do, say, think or feel as a result of this communication?

800. What are the dependencies?

801. When developing your communication plan do you address the following: When should the given message be communicated?

802. Will the culture embrace or reject this change?

803. Have the business unit contacts been briefed by the Virtual Desktop Infrastructure Monitoring project team?

804. What method and medium would you use to announce a message?

805. Is there an adequate supply of people for the new roles?

806. What are the responsibilities assigned to each role?

807. Identify the risk and assess the significance and likelihood of it occurring and plan the contingency What risks may occur upfront?

808. Is there support for this application(s) and are the details available for distribution?

809. How do you gain sponsors buy-in to the communication plan?

810. What are the needs, priorities and special interests of the audience?

811. Who is the audience for change management activities?

812. What would be an estimate of the total cost for the activities required to carry out the change initiative?

3.0 Executing Process Group: Virtual Desktop Infrastructure Monitoring

813. Who will be the main sponsor?

814. In what way has the programme come up with innovative measures for problem-solving?

815. Could a new application negatively affect the current IT infrastructure?

816. What are the main parts of the scope statement?

817. How can your organization use a weighted decision matrix to evaluate proposals as part of source selection?

818. What Virtual Desktop Infrastructure Monitoring projects and services are in the portfolio of your organization?

819. How can software assist in procuring goods and services?

820. It under budget or over budget?

821. What is in place for ensuring adequate change control on Virtual Desktop Infrastructure Monitoring projects that involve outside contracts?

822. When will the Virtual Desktop Infrastructure Monitoring project be done?

823. How do you prevent staff are just doing busywork to pass the time?

824. What is the shortest possible time it will take to complete this Virtual Desktop Infrastructure Monitoring project?

825. Does the Virtual Desktop Infrastructure Monitoring project team have the right skills?

826. How will professionals learn what is expected from them what the deliverables are?

827. What is the critical path for this Virtual Desktop Infrastructure Monitoring project and how long is it?

828. How can software assist in Virtual Desktop Infrastructure Monitoring project communications?

829. What were things that you need to improve?

830. How does Virtual Desktop Infrastructure Monitoring project management relate to other disciplines?

831. What were things that you did very well and want to do the same again on the next Virtual Desktop Infrastructure Monitoring project?

3.1 Team Member Status Report: Virtual Desktop Infrastructure Monitoring

832. How can you make it practical?

833. Do you have an Enterprise Virtual Desktop Infrastructure Monitoring project Management Office (EPMO)?

834. Does every department have to have a Virtual Desktop Infrastructure Monitoring project Manager on staff?

835. Are the organization's Virtual Desktop Infrastructure Monitoring projects more successful over time?

836. Are the attitudes of staff regarding Virtual Desktop Infrastructure Monitoring project work improving?

837. Why is it to be done?

838. How it is to be done?

839. Does the product, good, or service already exist within the organization?

840. The problem with Reward & Recognition Programs is that the truly deserving people all too often get left out. How can you make it practical?

841. Does the organization have the means (staff, money, contract, etc.) to produce or to acquire the product, good, or service?

842. Are the products of the organization's Virtual Desktop Infrastructure Monitoring projects meeting their customer's objectives?

843. Is there evidence that staff is taking a more professional approach toward management of the organizations Virtual Desktop Infrastructure Monitoring projects?

844. What specific interest groups do you have in place?

845. When a teams productivity and success depend on collaboration and the efficient flow of information, what generally fails them?

846. Will the staff do training or is that done by a third party?

847. How will Resource Planning be done?

848. How much risk is involved?

849. How does this product, good, or service meet the needs of the Virtual Desktop Infrastructure Monitoring project and the organization as a whole?

850. What is to be done?

3.2 Change Request: Virtual Desktop Infrastructure Monitoring

851. When Do you Create a Change Request?

852. How are changes requested (forms, method of communication)?

853. What is the relationship between requirements attributes and reliability?

854. Who is responsible to authorize changes?

855. What mechanism is used to appraise others of changes that are made?

856. What is the relationship between requirements attributes and attributes like complexity and size?

857. How does an organization control changes before and after software is released to a customer?

858. Why were my requested changes rejected or not made?

859. Who Will Perform the Change?

860. Have SCM procedures for noting the change, recording it, and reporting it been followed?

861. For which areas does this operating procedure apply?

862. Will all change requests be unconditionally tracked through this process?

863. What are the basic mechanics of the Change Advisory Board (CAB)?

864. What must be taken into consideration when introducing change control programs?

865. Are you Implementing ITIL Processes?

866. What are the Impacts to an organization?

867. Why control change across the life cycle?

868. Will there be a change request form in use?

869. Who can suggest changes?

870. Has a formal technical review been conducted to assess technical correctness?

3.3 Change Log: Virtual Desktop Infrastructure Monitoring

871. How does this relate to the standards developed for specific business processes?

872. How does this change affect scope?

873. How does this change affect the timeline of the schedule?

874. Is this a mandatory replacement?

875. Is the change backward compatible without limitations?

876. Do the described changes impact on the integrity or security of the system?

877. Is the submitted change a new change or a modification of a previously approved change?

878. Who initiated the change request?

879. Should a more thorough impact analysis be conducted?

880. Will the Virtual Desktop Infrastructure Monitoring project fail if the change request is not executed?

881. Is the requested change request a result of changes in other Virtual Desktop Infrastructure Monitoring project(s)?

882. Where Do Changes Come From?

883. Is the change request open, closed or pending?

884. Is the change request within Virtual Desktop Infrastructure Monitoring project scope?

885. When was the request approved?

886. When was the request submitted?

3.4 Decision Log: Virtual Desktop Infrastructure Monitoring

887. Is everything working as expected?

888. Who will be given a copy of this document and where will it be kept?

889. How consolidated and comprehensive a story can we tell by capturing currently available incident data in a central location and through a log of key decisions during an incident?

890. What makes you different or better than others companies selling the same thing?

891. Linked to original objective?

892. What eDiscovery problem or issue did your company set out to fix or make better?

893. Does anything need to be adjusted?

894. How does provision of information, both in terms of content and presentation, influence acceptance of alternative strategies?

895. What is the average size of your matters in an applicable measurement?

896. So, what is the line where eDiscovery ends and document review begins?

897. Adversarial Environment. Is your opponent open to a non-traditional workflow, or will it likely challenge anything you do?

898. Decision-making process; how will the team make decisions?

899. Which variables make a critical difference?

900. Meeting purpose; why does this team meet?

901. It becomes critical to track and periodically revisit both operational effectiveness; Are you noticing all that you need to, and are you interpreting what you see effectively?

902. How does the use a Decision Support System influence the strategies/tactics or costs?

903. How do you know when you are achieving it?

904. How do you define success?

905. At what point in time does loss become unacceptable?

906. Behaviors; what are guidelines that the team has identified that will assist them with getting the most out of their team meetings?

3.5 Quality Audit: Virtual Desktop Infrastructure Monitoring

907. Is refuse and garbage adequately stored and disposed of with sufficient frequency to prevent contamination?

908. How does the organization know that its security arrangements are appropriately effective and constructive?

909. How does the organization know that its support services planning and management systems are appropriately effective and constructive?

910. Statements of intent remain exactly that until they are put into effect. The next step is to deploy those intentions. In other words, do the plans happen in reality?

911. Are training programs documented?

912. Have the risks associated with the intentions been identified, analysed and appropriate responses developed?

913. How does your organization ensure that equipment is appropriately maintained and producing valid results?

914. Are adequate and conveniently located toilet facilities available for use by the employees?

915. Is the continuing professional education of key personnel explained in detail?

916. How does the organization know that its system for ensuring that its training activities are appropriately resourced and support is appropriately effective and constructive?

917. Is the process of self review, learning and improvement endemic throughout the organization?

918. How does the organization know that its relationships with industry and employers are appropriately effective and constructive?

919. How does your organization know that the review processes are effective?

920. How does the organization know that its public relations and marketing systems are appropriately effective and constructive?

921. Will the evidence likely be sufficient and appropriate?

922. Do the acceptance procedures and specifications include the criteria for acceptance/rejection, define the process to be used, and specify the measuring and test equipment that is to be used?

923. What are the main things that hinder your ability to do a good job?

924. What happens if our organization fails its Quality Audit?

925. Is there any content that may be legally actionable?

926. Have personnel cleanliness and health requirements been established?

3.6 Team Directory: Virtual Desktop Infrastructure Monitoring

927. What needs to be communicated?

928. How do unidentified risks impact the outcome of the Virtual Desktop Infrastructure Monitoring project?

929. Process Decisions: Are all start-up, turn over and close out requirements of the contract satisfied?

930. Contract requirements complied with?

931. Process Decisions: Are contractors adequately prosecuting the work?

932. What are you going to deliver or accomplish?

933. Process Decisions: How well was task order work performed?

934. Who will write the meeting minutes and distribute?

935. Process Decisions: Is work progressing on schedule and per contract requirements?

936. How will you accomplish and manage the objectives?

937. Who will be the stakeholders on your next Virtual Desktop Infrastructure Monitoring project?

938. Does a Virtual Desktop Infrastructure Monitoring project team directory list all resources assigned to the Virtual Desktop Infrastructure Monitoring project?

939. Who should receive information (all stakeholders)?

940. Why is the work necessary?

941. Process Decisions: Do invoice amounts match accepted work in place?

942. Who are the Team Members?

943. Do purchase specifications and configurations match requirements?

944. Is construction on schedule?

945. Timing: when do the effects of communication take place?

3.7 Team Operating Agreement: Virtual Desktop Infrastructure Monitoring

946. Are leadership responsibilities shared among team members (versus a single leader)?

947. Are there differences in access to communication and collaboration technology based on team member location?

948. Do you determine the meeting length and time of day?

949. What is a Virtual Team?

950. Methodologies: How will key team processes be implemented, such as training, research, work deliverable production, review and approval processes, knowledge management, and meeting procedures?

951. Are there the right people on your team?

952. The method to be used in the decision making process; Will it be consensus, majority rule, or the supervisor having the final say?

953. What is the number of cases currently teamed?

954. Must your team members rely on the expertise of other members to complete tasks?

955. What are the current caseload numbers in the unit?

956. What is Teaming?

957. Are team roles clearly defined and accepted?

958. Do you call or email participants to ensure understanding, follow-through and commitment to the meeting outcomes?

959. Must your members collaborate successfully to complete Virtual Desktop Infrastructure Monitoring projects?

960. Are there more than two functional areas represented by your team?

961. Do you send out the agenda and meeting materials in advance?

962. Resource Allocation: How will individual team members account for their time and expenses, and how will this be allocated in the team budget?

963. Do team members reside in more than two countries?

964. Is compensation based on team and individual performance?

965. Have you set the goals and objectives of the team?

3.8 Team Performance Assessment: Virtual Desktop Infrastructure Monitoring

966. To what degree are the teams goals and objectives clear, simple, and measurable?

967. What makes opportunities more or less obvious?

968. Do you give group members authority to make at least some important decisions?

969. To what degree will the team ensure that all members equitably share the work essential to the success of the team?

970. To what degree will new and supplemental skills be introduced as the need is recognized?

971. To what degree are the goals realistic?

972. To what degree will the approach capitalize on and enhance the skills of all team members in a manner that takes into consideration other demands on members of the team?

973. Do you promptly inform members about major developments that may affect them?

974. To what degree will the team adopt a concrete, clearly understood, and agreed-upon approach that will result in achievement of the teams goals?

975. To what degree does the teams purpose contain themes that are particularly meaningful and memorable?

976. Where to from here?

977. To what degree do the goals specify concrete team work products?

978. To what degree can team members vigorously define the teams purpose in discussions with others who are not part of the functioning team?

979. To what degree are staff involved as partners in the improvement process?

980. To what degree do team members frequently explore the teams purpose and its implications?

981. To what degree does the teams work approach provide opportunity for members to engage in fact-based problem solving?

982. To what degree are the goals ambitious?

983. What structural changes have you made or are you preparing to make?

984. To what degree do all members feel responsible for all agreed-upon measures?

985. To what degree do members understand and articulate the same purpose without relying on ambiguous abstractions?

3.9 Team Member Performance Assessment: Virtual Desktop Infrastructure Monitoring

986. Is it critical or vital to the job?

987. How do you implement Cost Reduction?

988. Goals met?

989. What qualities does a successful Team leader possess?

990. How was the determination made for which training platforms would be used (i.e., media selection)?

991. To what degree do team members articulate the teams work approach?

992. To what degree can the team measure progress against specific goals?

993. How are evaluation results utilized?

994. How is assessment information achieved, stored?

995. Do the goals support the organizations goals?

996. Does statute or regulation require the job responsibility?

997. What kinds of performance factors / elements do

we use?

998. To what degree can team members meet frequently enough to accomplish the teams ends?

999. What steps have you taken to improve performance?

1000. To what degree do team members feel that the purpose of the team is important, if not exciting?

1001. How is performance assessment used in making future award decisions including options and extend/compete decisions?

1002. How do you know that all team members are learning?

3.10 Issue Log: Virtual Desktop Infrastructure Monitoring

1003. What is a Stakeholder?

1004. What is the stakeholders political influence?

1005. Why Multiple Evaluators?

1006. What would have to change?

1007. How Do you Manage Human Resources?

1008. Who are the members of the governing body?

1009. Who were proponents/opponents?

1010. What does the stakeholder need from the team?

1011. Do you feel more overwhelmed by stakeholders?

1012. Are the Virtual Desktop Infrastructure Monitoring project Issues uniquely identified, including to which product they refer?

1013. Is access to the Issue Log controlled?

1014. Which stakeholders are thought leaders, influences, or early adopters?

1015. Do you feel a register helps?

1016. Who have you worked with in past, similar initiatives?

1017. Do you often overlook a key stakeholder or stakeholder group?

1018. Are the stakeholders getting the information they need, are they consulted, are their concerns addressed?

1019. How do you reply to this question; I am new here and managing this major program. How do you suggest I build my network?

4.0 Monitoring and Controlling Process Group: Virtual Desktop Infrastructure Monitoring

1020. If no change, where should you look for problems?

1021. Is there adequate validation on required fields?

1022. What areas were overlooked on this Virtual Desktop Infrastructure Monitoring project?

1023. What resources (both financial and non-financial) are available/needed?

1024. Propriety: Who needs to be involved in the evaluation to be ethical?

1025. How well did the chosen processes fit the needs of the Virtual Desktop Infrastructure Monitoring project?

1026. What kinds of things in particular are you looking for data on?

1027. Accuracy: What design will lead to accurate information?

1028. How well defined and documented were the Virtual Desktop Infrastructure Monitoring project management processes you chose to use?

1029. How to ensure validity, quality and consistency?

1030. How can you make your needs known?

1031. Who are the Virtual Desktop Infrastructure Monitoring project stakeholders?

1032. Did the Virtual Desktop Infrastructure Monitoring project team have enough people to execute the Virtual Desktop Infrastructure Monitoring project plan?

1033. What factors are contributing to progress or delay in the achievement of products and results?

1034. What input will you be required to provide the Virtual Desktop Infrastructure Monitoring project team?

1035. Is there undesirable impact on staff or resources?

1036. If action is called for, what form should it take?

1037. Overall, how does the program function to serve the clients?

4.1 Project Performance Report: Virtual Desktop Infrastructure Monitoring

1038. What is the PRS?

1039. To what degree does the information network communicate information relevant to the task?

1040. To what degree are the team's goals and objectives clear, simple, and measurable?

1041. To what degree does the team's work approach provide opportunity for members to engage in fact-based problem solving?

1042. How is the data used?

1043. To what degree do the relationships of the informal organization motivate task- relevant behavior and facilitate task completion?

1044. To what degree are the structures of the formal organization consistent with the behaviors in the informal organization?

1045. To what degree does the team's work approach provide opportunity for members to engage in open interaction?

1046. To what degree does the formal organization make use of individual resources and meet individual needs?

1047. To what degree does the team's approach to its work allow for modification and improvement over time?

1048. To what degree will each member have the opportunity to advance his or her professional skills in all three of the above categories while contributing to the accomplishment of the team's purpose and goals?

1049. To what degree do team members frequently explore the team's purpose and its implications?

1050. To what degree are the skill areas critical to team performance present?

1051. To what degree are the demands of the task compatible with and converge with the mission and functions of the formal organization?

1052. To what degree do team members agree with the goals, their relative importance, and the ways in which their achievement will be measured?

1053. How will procurement be coordinated with other Virtual Desktop Infrastructure Monitoring project aspects, such as scheduling and performance reporting?

1054. To what degree does the team's work approach provide opportunity for members to engage in results-based evaluation?

1055. To what degree can all members engage in open and interactive discussions?

4.2 Variance Analysis: Virtual Desktop Infrastructure Monitoring

1056. Wbs elements contractually specified for reporting of status to the organization (lowest level only)?

1057. Are overhead costs budgets established on a basis consistent with the anticipated direct business base?

1058. What is the total budget for the Virtual Desktop Infrastructure Monitoring project (including estimates for authorized but unpriced work)?

1059. Are the organizations and items of cost assigned to each pool identified?

1060. Are significant decision points, constraints, and interfaces identified as key milestones?

1061. How does the organization allocate the cost of shared expenses and services?

1062. Are material costs reported within the same period as that in which BCWP is earned for that material?

1063. How do you identify and isolate causes of favorable and unfavorable cost and schedule variances?

1064. Are the WBS and organizational levels for

application of the Virtual Desktop Infrastructure Monitoring projected overhead costs identified?

1065. What can be the cause of an increase in costs?

1066. What is your organizations rationale for sharing expenses and services between business segments?

1067. Contract line items and end items?

1068. When, during the last four quarters, did a primary business event occur causing a fluctuation?

1069. Are there quarterly budgets with quarterly performance comparisons?

1070. Are the bases and rates for allocating costs from each indirect pool consistently applied?

1071. Favorable or Unfavorable Variance?

1072. Is the entire contract planned in time-phased control accounts to the extent practicable?

1073. Can Process Improvements Lead to Unfavorable Variances?

4.3 Earned Value Status: Virtual Desktop Infrastructure Monitoring

1074. Are you hitting your Virtual Desktop Infrastructure Monitoring projects targets?

1075. Validation is a process of ensuring that the developed system will actually achieve the stakeholders desired outcomes; Are you building the right product? What do you validate?

1076. When is it going to finish?

1077. If earned value management (EVM) is so good in determining the true status of a Virtual Desktop Infrastructure Monitoring project and Virtual Desktop Infrastructure Monitoring project its completion, why is it that hardly any one uses it in information systems related Virtual Desktop Infrastructure Monitoring projects?

1078. How does this compare with other Virtual Desktop Infrastructure Monitoring projects?

1079. Where are your problem areas?

1080. Earned Value can be used in almost any Virtual Desktop Infrastructure Monitoring project situation and in almost any Virtual Desktop Infrastructure Monitoring project environment. It may be used on large Virtual Desktop Infrastructure Monitoring projects, medium sized Virtual Desktop Infrastructure Monitoring projects, tiny Virtual Desktop

Infrastructure Monitoring projects (in cut-down form), complex and simple Virtual Desktop Infrastructure Monitoring projects and in any market sector. Some people, of course, know all about earned value, they have used it for years - but perhaps not as effectively as they could have?

1081. What is the unit of forecast value?

1082. Where is Evidence-based Earned Value in your organization reported?

1083. How much is it going to cost by the finish?

1084. Verification is a process of ensuring that the developed system satisfies the stakeholders agreements and specifications; Are you building the product right? What do you verify?

4.4 Risk Audit: Virtual Desktop Infrastructure Monitoring

1085. Has risk management been considered when planning an event?

1086. Does the customer have a solid idea of what is required?

1087. Is Risk an management agenda item?

1088. Have you considered the health and safety of everyone in the organization and do you meet work health and safety regulations?

1089. Extending the discussion on the halo effect, to what extent are auditors able to build skepticism in evidence review?

1090. What impact does experience with one client have on decisions made for other clients during the risk-assessment process?

1091. Do you have a clear plan for the future that describes what you want to do and how you are going to do it?

1092. Strategic business risk audit methodologies; are these an attempt to sell other services, and is management becoming the client of the audit rather than the shareholder?

1093. What are the outcomes you are looking for?

1094. How effective are your risk controls?

1095. What can you do to manage outcomes?

1096. Will an appropriate standard of care be applied to all involved?

1097. Are policies communicated to all affected?

1098. Does the implementation method matter?

1099. Does your auditor understand your business?

1100. Whence the business risk audit?

1101. Does your organization have a process for meeting its ongoing taxation obligations?

1102. Do you conduct risk assessments on all programs, activities and events?

1103. Have customers been involved fully in the definition of requirements?

1104. Have all involved been advised of any obligations they have to sponsors?

4.5 Contractor Status Report: Virtual Desktop Infrastructure Monitoring

1105. What process manages the contracts?

1106. What was the budget or estimated cost for your companys services?

1107. What was the overall budget or estimated cost?

1108. What was the actual budget or estimated cost for your companys services?

1109. Describe how often regular updates are made to the proposed solution. Are these regular updates included in the standard maintenance plan?

1110. What is the average response time for answering a support call?

1111. If applicable; describe your standard schedule for new software version releases. Are new software version releases included in the standard maintenance plan?

1112. How is Risk Transferred?

1113. What are the minimum and optimal bandwidth requirements for the proposed soluiton?

1114. How long have you been using the services?

1115. What was the final actual cost?

1116. Are there contractual transfer concerns?

1117. Who can list a Virtual Desktop Infrastructure Monitoring project as company experience, the company or a previous employee of the company?

4.6 Formal Acceptance: Virtual Desktop Infrastructure Monitoring

1118. Was the Virtual Desktop Infrastructure Monitoring project managed well?

1119. Was the Virtual Desktop Infrastructure Monitoring project work done on time, within budget, and according to specification?

1120. Have all comments been addressed?

1121. What are the requirements against which to test, Who will execute?

1122. Who would use it?

1123. Who supplies data?

1124. What function(s) does it fill or meet?

1125. How does your team plan to obtain formal acceptance on your Virtual Desktop Infrastructure Monitoring project?

1126. Was the client satisfied with the Virtual Desktop Infrastructure Monitoring project results?

1127. What lessons were learned about your Virtual Desktop Infrastructure Monitoring project management methodology?

1128. Did the Virtual Desktop Infrastructure

Monitoring project manager and team act in a professional and ethical manner?

1129. Do you perform formal acceptance or burn-in tests?

1130. Is formal acceptance of the Virtual Desktop Infrastructure Monitoring project product documented and distributed?

1131. Do you buy-in installation services?

1132. Was the sponsor/customer satisfied?

1133. Was the Virtual Desktop Infrastructure Monitoring project goal achieved?

1134. What can you do better next time?

1135. How well did the team follow the methodology?

1136. Does it do what client said it would?

1137. Does it do what Virtual Desktop Infrastructure Monitoring project team said it would?

5.0 Closing Process Group: Virtual Desktop Infrastructure Monitoring

1138. Was the schedule met?

1139. What areas does the group agree are the biggest success on the Virtual Desktop Infrastructure Monitoring project?

1140. What were things that you did very well and want to do the same again on the next Virtual Desktop Infrastructure Monitoring project?

1141. What could have been improved?

1142. When will the Virtual Desktop Infrastructure Monitoring project be done?

1143. How Well Did You Do?

1144. Can the lesson learned be replicated?

1145. Were risks identified and mitigated?

1146. What could be done to improve the process?

1147. Did you do what you said you were going to do?

1148. What is the Virtual Desktop Infrastructure Monitoring project Management Process?

1149. Is the Virtual Desktop Infrastructure Monitoring project Funded?

1150. Contingency planning. If a risk event occurs, what will you do?

1151. Just how important is your work to the overall success of the Virtual Desktop Infrastructure Monitoring project?

1152. What went well?

1153. What Business Situation Is Being Addressed?

1154. What is the risk of failure to the organization?

1155. How well did the chosen processes produce the expected results?

5.1 Procurement Audit: Virtual Desktop Infrastructure Monitoring

1156. Are there procedures governing the negotiations of long-term contracts?

1157. In case of time and material and labour hour contracts, does surveillance give an adequate and reasonable assurance that the contractor is using efficient methods and effective cost controls?

1158. Does the procurement function/unit have the ability to secure best performance from contractors?

1159. Are all initial purchase contracts made by the purchasing organization?

1160. Are the official minutes written in a clear and concise manner?

1161. Has alternatives been considered for the specified procurement Virtual Desktop Infrastructure Monitoring project?

1162. Relevance of the contract to the Internal Market?

1163. Is the company policy on purchasing covered by a written manual?

1164. What are your procurement processes with contractors?

1165. Were no charges billed to interested economic operators or the parties to the system?

1166. Are risks in the external environment identified, for example: Budgetary constraints?

1167. Proper and complete records of transactions and events are maintained?

1168. Are the number of checking accounts where cash segregation is not required kept to a reasonable number?

1169. Is the organization transparent about winning bids and prices?

1170. Does each policy statement contain the legal reference(s) on which the policy is based?

1171. Is the weighting set coherent, convincing and leaving little scope for arbitrary and random evaluation and ranking?

1172. Is an employee assigned to follow up at regular intervals on outstanding purchase orders over 30 days old?

1173. Is there a form specified for bids?

1174. Did the chosen procedure ensure competition and transparency?

1175. Are internal control mechanisms performed before payments?

5.2 Contract Close-Out: Virtual Desktop Infrastructure Monitoring

1176. Parties: Who is Involved?

1177. Was the contract sufficiently clear so as not to result in numerous disputes and misunderstandings?

1178. Are the signers the authorized officials?

1179. A change in knowledge?

1180. Have all contract records been included in the Virtual Desktop Infrastructure Monitoring project archives?

1181. Has each contract been audited to verify acceptance and delivery?

1182. How/When Used ?

1183. What is Capture Management?

1184. A change in attitude or behavior?

1185. How is the contracting office notified of the automatic contract close-out?

1186. What happens to the recipient of services?

1187. Have all acceptance criteria been met prior to final payment to contractors?

1188. Was the contract type appropriate?

1189. Have all contracts been completed?

1190. Have all contracts been closed?

1191. Was the contract complete without requiring numerous changes and revisions?

1192. Parties: Authorized?

1193. A change in circumstances?

1194. Why Outsource?

1195. How does it work?

5.3 Project or Phase Close-Out: Virtual Desktop Infrastructure Monitoring

1196. Planned Remaining Costs?

1197. What are the mandatory communication needs for each stakeholder?

1198. Does the lesson educate others to improve performance?

1199. Who are the Virtual Desktop Infrastructure Monitoring project stakeholders and what are their roles and involvement?

1200. What advantages do the an individual interview have over a group meeting, and vice-versa?

1201. Who exerted influence that has positively affected or negatively impacted the Virtual Desktop Infrastructure Monitoring project?

1202. What information is each stakeholder group interested in?

1203. What was expected from each stakeholder?

1204. What is this stakeholder expecting?

1205. What Security Considerations needed to be addressed during the Procurement Life Cycle?

1206. What are the marketing communication needs

for each stakeholder?

1207. What stakeholder group needs, expectations, and interests are being met by the Virtual Desktop Infrastructure Monitoring project?

1208. How often did each stakeholder need an update?

1209. If you were the Virtual Desktop Infrastructure Monitoring project sponsor, how would you determine which Virtual Desktop Infrastructure Monitoring project team(s) and/or individuals deserve recognition?

1210. In preparing the Lessons Learned report, should it reflect a consensus viewpoint, or should the report reflect the different individual viewpoints?

1211. What hierarchical authority does the stakeholder have in the organization?

1212. Is the lesson significant, valid, and applicable?

5.4 Lessons Learned: Virtual Desktop Infrastructure Monitoring

1213. What is the proportion of in-house and contractor personnel authorized for the Virtual Desktop Infrastructure Monitoring project?

1214. Were the Virtual Desktop Infrastructure Monitoring project goals attained?

1215. What was the geopolitical history during the origin of the organization and at the time of task input?

1216. How effective were the communications materials in providing and orienting team members about the details of the Virtual Desktop Infrastructure Monitoring project?

1217. What things surprised you on the Virtual Desktop Infrastructure Monitoring project that were not in the plan?

1218. What would you like to see better documented about how to use existing processes on this type of Virtual Desktop Infrastructure Monitoring project?

1219. How well were expectations met regarding the frequency and content of information that was conveyed to by the Virtual Desktop Infrastructure Monitoring project Manager?

1220. How useful was the content of the training you

received in preparation for the use of the product/service?

1221. Did the delivered product meet the specified requirements and goals of the Virtual Desktop Infrastructure Monitoring project?

1222. How efficient were Virtual Desktop Infrastructure Monitoring project team meetings conducted?

1223. How was the quality of products/processes assured?

1224. How effectively were issues managed on the Virtual Desktop Infrastructure Monitoring project?

1225. Did the Virtual Desktop Infrastructure Monitoring project change significantly?

1226. How effective were Best Practices & Lessons Learned from prior Virtual Desktop Infrastructure Monitoring projects utilized in this Virtual Desktop Infrastructure Monitoring project?

1227. How satisfied are you with your involvement in the development and/or review of the Virtual Desktop Infrastructure Monitoring project Scope during Virtual Desktop Infrastructure Monitoring project Initiation and Planning?

1228. Did the Virtual Desktop Infrastructure Monitoring project improve the team members reputations, skills, personal development?

1229. Recommendation: What do you recommend

should be done to ensure that others throughout the organization can benefit from what you have learned?

1230. How timely were Progress Reports provided to the Virtual Desktop Infrastructure Monitoring project Manager by Team Members?

1231. Is there any way in which you think our development process hampered this Virtual Desktop Infrastructure Monitoring project?

1232. What skills did you need that were missing on this Virtual Desktop Infrastructure Monitoring project?

Index

Lightning Source UK Ltd.
Milton Keynes UK
UKHW02f0131121018
330406UK00004B/35/P